2:52
Learning to Grow On Purpose

lessons from Jesus' hidden years

JOHN ANDREWS

RIVER
PUBLISHING

River Publishing & Media Ltd
www.river-publishing.co.uk

info@river-publishing.co.uk

ISBN 978-1-908393-25-8

Revised and updated edition.
Copyright © John Andrews 2020

Printed in the United Kingdom

Contents

Acknowledgements

My name is on the cover, but so many have invested into both myself and this project allowing this, my tenth book, an opportunity to speak. Words seem inadequate in expressing my deepest thanks to all those who have helped make me the person I am today. I am better because of you. Thank you, thank you, thank you!

However, special thanks must go to the following people:

To Dawn, (my Delicious one), for your tireless and selfless service of our family and for your love and patience that empowers me to write. Your sacrifice is unquantifiable and your reward will be unimaginable. I could not do it without you.

To Elaina, Simeon and Beth-Anne who have taught me more about myself than you will ever know. As you grow on purpose you will live in power.

Thanks goes to Paul "Blue Forever" Reid who kindly wrote the foreword for this book. Paul, you and Pricilla have enriched our lives immensely since coming into them. My only regret is that it took so long for us to connect. Thanks for everything.

Thanks to Joy for your assistance with proofing the manuscript.

To Tim Pettingale for (again) expertly helping me to get a book into print and to River Publishing for believing in my dreams.

Finally, to my Heavenly Father, for your relentless loving commitment to "project Andrews". I am continuously overwhelmed by what You have done for me, given me and prepared for me. I know that Your purpose for my life is great and I want to always honour that by learning to grow on purpose and live ready. Thank You!

Foreword

"I'd like to do what you do," said the young man in my study, "preaching that is, how long will it take?"

I've been asked that many times and my reply is always the same: 10,000 hours! My old mentor used to say, "for every hour in the pulpit, ten hours preparation."

I love John's new book as I have never, ever read one dedicated to the "hidden" years of Jesus. His glorious three years of public ministry were preceded by a life of learning and faithful service.

John argues articulately from the few passages that we have on "the first thirty years" that the life of Christ was one of continual learning, steady growth and discipleship. He was a real man, He faced many of the same things we do and "Son though He was, He learned obedience by the things He suffered." John reasons that if the Son of God had to go through the process of daily discipleship then so do we!

I love this book because it's not a quick-fix solution to becoming a disciple of Jesus; no ten easy steps, but a lifelong commitment of learning to be spiritual.

John's insights into the passages are enlightening and his comments are profound and challenging. He encourages us to think and work hard.

His summary of Malcolm Gladwell in chapter two is powerful:

Talent + preparation + opportunity = achievement.

Not only does it motivate us, through Scripture, to a lifetime of discipleship and how we can best begin this journey but it is full of practical guidance that, if followed, will prove invaluable in moving the convert to becoming a disciple.

However, I love this book best because it reflects John's own journey and embodies the truth of one of his own quotes:

**Nothing is truly taught until something is learned
Nothing is truly learned until it is lived.**

In one sense it is his own story – a life of discipleship and learning. He has lived what he is writing about and it is all the more potent for that.

We are always looking for material that will help converts become disciples and I for one will be handing this book out to those who are committed to that lifelong journey.

Paul Reid
CFC, Belfast 2012

1. Ready, Steady, Go!

It is easy to fall into the temptation of thinking that when it comes to the earthly ministry of Jesus, He simply appeared at the age of 30 and started to do what He did. Considering we have four writers who record and report the life of Jesus, we have relatively little detail of His life up to the commencement of His ministry. Only Matthew and Luke give some insights, but even these are sparse. We know the names of Jesus' father, mother and four brothers (though not His sisters);(1) we know where His family eventually settled down and lived (2) and we know that at the age of 12 He had an interesting experience with both teachers and parents in the Temple (3). Beyond this we know very little. However, what all the gospel writers agree on is that at a certain moment, Jesus appeared. Look at how each describes this glorious appearing:

At that time Jesus came from Nazareth in Galilee and was baptized by John in the Jordan. Mark 1:9

Then Jesus came from Galilee to the Jordan to be baptized by John. Matthew 3:13

When all the people were being baptized, Jesus was baptized too. Luke 3:21

The next day John saw Jesus coming toward him and said, "Look, the Lamb of God, who takes away the sin of the world..." John 1:29

Once Jesus appears, the danger is that all that has gone before is at worst forgotten, or at best pushed into the background. We want to get to His miracle-laden ministry, His teaching on the Kingdom and of course His death and resurrection. From the moment of His appearing, our natural inclination is to look forward at what is about to happen, not look back at what has been. For approximately three years Jesus impacted His world and even now, 2,000 years later, though I've read the gospels hundreds of times, those three short years of ministry still mesmerise me! But these three years represent only 9% of the life of Jesus on earth... what about the other 91%? This 91% incorporates the silent years of Jesus, yet undoubtedly they form the foundation for the 9% for which Jesus is most famously remembered and celebrated.

I love how the Bible in a few short verses can summarise years of time. What takes me just a couple of minutes to read may have taken someone 50 years to live. We see this in the life of Jesus. At the end of Luke chapter 2 we're told that Jesus went home to Nazareth where He grew. But 21 verses later we're told that Jesus was baptized by John in the Jordan. Those 21 verses took me less than a minute to read, but took Jesus 18 years to live! Yet, how quickly I skip over those years and verses in order to get to the "real" action of the story.

In recent years I have been drawn to mediate and learn from the 91% of Jesus' life, largely hidden but delightfully illuminated by Dr Luke. He gives us just enough to show us that the 91% is important and vital if we are to follow the example of Jesus, but he does not give us too much that might cause us to fixate on a child prodigy and miss the Messiah. Though as a follower and leader I continue to delve into the magnificent 9% of Jesus' life, I admit that I have also become a student of the 91% and an advocate of what I have come to call simply *the 2:52 principle.*

Luke tells us:

And Jesus grew in wisdom and stature, and in favour with God and men. Luke 2:52

Twice in the early pre-ministry years of Jesus, Luke tells us, He grew. In 2:40 the implication is of Jesus' growth during the tender years of His childhood, and here in 2:52 Luke implies that from 12 years old onwards this becomes the code by which Jesus lived. In short, through these two little pinpricks of light into the 91%,

Luke tells us that these are the "growing years" of Jesus and it is on this premise that the principles of this book are built. If Jesus grew, I want to know how He grew, why He grew and in what areas He grew. If He grew, then how much more should I, as one who aspires both to follow Him and to lead others, take my life-growth seriously? It's a sobering thought that without the 91% the 9% would never have happened. Each of the gospel writers tell us that Jesus appeared and that He was ready when He did so... but it is only Luke, through the lens of 2:52, who tells us why Jesus was ready to go! So, why was Jesus ready? Even from the tiny crumbs of information we have, I can suggest the following reasons why Jesus was ready.

He excelled in the ordinary

Then He went down to Nazareth with them and was obedient to them... (Luke 2:51)

Such a simple, straightforward statement, easily missed in the rush to His appearance, contains the kernel of greatness, especially when we consider the context of both His actions and His home.

Note the first phrase within this verse: "...He went down to Nazareth with them..."

The reason He went down is because He had been up in Jerusalem. The city itself is about 2,500 feet above sea level, so one literally goes up to Jerusalem. Then, within the city, the Temple was elevated and each section within the temple was higher than the next until the Holy of Holies was, in reality, the highest place in the city. But Jesus wasn't just going down at a geographic level; think of His emotional, spiritual and psychological descent. He had just spent 3 days (without His parents), arguing and debating with the teachers of the Law. Jesus had become so engrossed that perhaps He had lost track of time. But now He has to leave the Temple, leave the buzz of debate, leave the pulse of one of the greatest cities on earth and return to the north, to a village of less than 300 inhabitants, a village off the beaten track of the main trading routes of the day, a village so small and insignificant that it wasn't even on the map of His own 1st century world! How easy it is to read the phrase that He went down, but I suggest to you that this was a deeply costly journey.

Now note the second phrase in this verse, "…and was obedient to them…"

The word translated obedient is *hupotássō* and is two words joined together. *Hupo* means "under" and *tássō*, "to order". Together they suggest that Jesus was "under orders", that He literally placed Himself under the authority and order of His parents. Now this is even more remarkable when we remember what He in fact had said to His parents at the Temple:

"Why were you searching for Me? Didn't you know I had to be in My Father's house?"(4)

The text makes it clear that they didn't understand what Jesus was talking about, but He did. Yet, even though He knew who He was, the significance of the place where He sat, and the reason He was there, He still voluntarily submitted Himself to be under the orders of His earthly parents!

In the New Testament, there are two words often translated time or season. One word is *chrónos* and denotes the idea of space or time regardless of length. This word is used by Paul, for example, in Galatians when he talks of Jesus being born of a woman *"when the time had fully come…"*(5). But then there is another word, *kairós*, which denotes more of the idea of a season of time, or time that carries special meaning or purpose, and throughout the New Testament has been translated as "proper time", "right time" and "appointed time".(6) I think this is what we see here in the life of Jesus when thinking about the tension between the 91% & 9%. Jesus lives well in the chrónos moments so that when the kairós opportunity arises He is prepared and ready. He learns to grow in the chrónos so that He can minister in the kairós. He works as hard in the chrónos when no one is really paying attention as He does in the kairós when everyone wants a piece of Him. He is able to step into His "one day" – kairós, because He learned to live well in the "every day" – chrónos.

So many people love the idea of God's kairós for them – that *one day*, that suddenly moment when they will be propelled into the limelight of God's purpose and all eyes will be on them. But if such a day is ever going to happen, then each of us must take the ordinary, routine and sometimes mundane "every days" seriously and we must learn to live well in our chrónos moments. On my laptop I can take what's known as a screen-shot. In effect, the computer takes a still picture of whatever is on my screen, thus freezing it for me. How many times have we been guilty of a screen-shot mentality when it comes to a marriage, a successful person, a home, a business or even a church or ministry? We look at them, snap in our minds and wish our lives resembled theirs in some small way. But the danger with the screen-shot is that it ignores all that has gone before. In other words, we love the picture... but aren't too keen on the process! To help us to avoid this common and potentially catastrophic mistake, Dr Luke doesn't just show us Jesus turning up enjoying His kairós, but cleverly gives us a glimpse of something of how Jesus' chrónos might have looked. He helps us understand that the magnificence of the 9% owes much of its success to the extra-ordinariness of the 91%. I sometimes define extraordinary as "someone doing the ordinary really well, a lot". Jesus lived under the orders of His human parents, He lived in a small, obscure backwater village, He lived a largely misunderstood or non-understood life... but He lived well, excelling in the ordinary! I submit to you that in "doing the ordinary, really well, a lot", Jesus maximized His chrónos and was therefore ready to capitalize on God's kairós!

He embraced responsibility

Isn't this the carpenter? Isn't this Mary's son and the brother of James, Joseph, Judas and Simon? Aren't His sisters here with us? And they took offence at Him. Mark 6:3

Why did they take offence at Him? The usual interpretation is because of His teaching delivered that Sabbath in the Synagogue, and of course that is part of it. But the key to getting to the heart of the offence is contained in verse 2:

"Where did this man get these things? What's this wisdom that has been given Him, that He even does miracles?"

They couldn't get over how someone so ordinary, someone who was part of their community, could suddenly become so different, so gifted, so clever! This is further confirmed by the terms in which they describe Him.

"Isn't this the carpenter..."

His trade. The word used here is *tékton* and is used predominantly of workers in wood, though it can be applied to craftsmen of other sorts, such as masons, sculptors or smiths. In a small village the *tékton* would need to be versatile, able to deal both with agricultural and other implements and also with the construction and repair of buildings. As such he was a significant figure in the village economy, probably also undertaking skilled work in the surrounding area. In this context, then, there is nothing derogatory in the term.(7)

"Isn't this Mary's son…"

His leadership within the family. Mark's gospel doesn't make a single reference to Joseph and the fact that he shares that Jesus was the "son of Mary" implies that Joseph was not only already dead, but as the eldest son, Jesus had assumed leadership of the home and the chief responsibility to oversee provision for His family.

"… and the brother of… aren't His sisters here with us…"

His family context. The fact that He's identified with His family is an indicator that up until leaving home to begin His ministry, Jesus had in fact remained at home around His mother, brothers and sisters.

The people see Jesus the only way they know how, in the context of His responsibilities. Up until this moment, Jesus had been a good craftsman and no doubt many within the village had benefited from His expertise. On Joseph's passing, Jesus became the "man of the house" and took care of Mary and His siblings. Even though He was 30, He remained unmarried and never moved away from the family home. Jesus was the model of domestic and filial responsibility… that's why when He taught so brilliantly at the synagogue it was a shock and why so many dismissed what He had to say.

Ever wondered why Jesus connected so well to peasant-dominated culture?

…Because He lived among them.

Ever wondered why He was so tender to widows and used them so often in His stories?

…Because His mother was one.

Ever wondered why the ordinary felt so comfortable around Him?

...Because He was just like them.

Jesus didn't have the luxury to live and train with the elite, or concentrate on His Torah studies without the distraction of domestic pressure. Instead He learned and grew in the ordinary places of life. He understood the pressure of taxation, family budgets and oppression. He managed the tension of the promises of God contained in the Scriptures while living as an exiled 2nd class citizen in His own land.

During the 91% Jesus didn't run from responsibility; He embraced it, learned from it and mastered it. When He stood on the hillside and said, *"Blessed are the poor in spirit..."*, He did so as one with hands toughened by toil, compassion shaped by hardship and with a theology tried and tested in reality. Ironically for His hometown, the disguise of His domestic responsibility became a hindrance to them hearing His words, when for the masses the authenticity of the tékton Rabbi was one of the reasons they found Him so attractive.

In *Visioneering*, Andy Stanley asks the questions:

"Why should God bring an opportunity your way if you are not in a position to take advantage of it? If you were God, to whom would you give opportunities? Wishful thinkers? Dreamers? Or planners?"(8)

Jesus didn't live in a dream, waiting for his kairós opportunity, instead He invested His energy, creativity and ability into the ordinary of His chrónos moments. If He could run a business, then maybe He could lead a movement. If He loved His mother, then maybe He'd be able to engage with the margins. If He served His family, then maybe He could serve His nation. If He could make life work when nobody noticed, then maybe, just maybe, He could show the world how life was meant to work when all eyes were on Him!

He understood His destiny

Didn't you know I had to be in My Father's house. Luke 2:49

I believe the religious upbringing Jesus would have been exposed to was a key factor in helping Him discover not only who He was but why He was here. For many Christians it is hard to entertain the idea that Jesus didn't know everything and that at multiple levels He may have had to learn. Though they accept that Jesus was fully human and fully God (for me the most mysterious of all mysteries), most will want to believe that the God-part informed the human part and therefore Jesus knew everything before He ever learned to speak Hebrew. As you may have guessed, I fundamentally disagree with this and I think Dr Luke wants us to see that although Jesus was "very God of very God", as a man, He still had to learn. The strong commitment to learning the Scriptures in the 1st Century Jewish world, I believe, became a guide to the young Jesus. The Mishnah describes the education process that would have been typical of many young men at the time of Jesus.(9)

At five years old – one is fit for the Scripture. Children were encouraged to read and memorise the Torah and other parts of the Tanakh.(10)

At ten years old – Oral Torah. These were the interpretations of the Torah handed down by various Rabbis or teachers.

At thirteen years old – fulfilling the commandments. At this point formal study ended and they would begin to learn a trade. The more talented young men would be encouraged to study further at the "house of interpretation" (*bet midrash*) at the synagogue, until they were married at eighteen or twenty.

At eighteen – the bridal chamber. If they were going to get married this would normally be the time, remembering it was an expectation, not a requirement.

At twenty years old – the pursuit of a vocation.

At thirty years old – the authority to teach others.(11)

I believe somewhere in all this learning, Jesus discovered who He was and why He was here, and therefore at the age of 12, He was able to confidently proclaim it to His family, even though at that moment, they didn't get it. A 12-year old in Western 21st Century culture is someone just beginning teenage years, having just left childhood, but in the world of Jesus, one left childhood and became a man in a single day. As Jesus sat in the Temple debating, arguing and asking (note that, asking), He wasn't there as a lost child, but as a young man. It is striking that during the first few days of His newly acquired adult status, Jesus made a clear declaration that He understood His personhood and His purpose!

The danger here is that we pass this off glibly with a "well that's Jesus", thus missing the power of this moment. From the age of 5 to 12, Jesus had so engaged with God's written instruction, the Torah, that He had come to an understanding of who God was, what God wanted and how He fitted into the plan. Today we argue such maturity is not possible from children and young people and many churches entertain young people instead of taking this truth seriously and beginning a dedicated process of educating them in Truth. The sooner young minds engage in a life-giving way with the Truth contained in God's word, the quicker they will discover their personhood and purpose. The devil knows that our God-given purpose is linked to our God-created identity and thus is doing all he can to distort one in order to destroy the other. In the 91% Jesus gave energy to asking the BIG questions. *Who is God and what does He want? Who am I and why am I here?* At 12 He had worked it out... and note the reaction to Him. The teachers and people who heard Him "were amazed" and His parents "were astonished".

If like Jesus we can ask the BIG questions:

Who is God and what does He want?

Who am I and why am I here?

And if like Jesus we can find the answers to them, sooner rather than later, we will, like Him, both amaze and astonish our world!

He grew deliberately

And Jesus grew in wisdom and stature, and in favour with God and men. Luke 2:52

In concluding this chapter, I wanted to return to the verse that forms the pulse of this book. In bringing this episode at the Temple to a close, Luke leaves us with the singular thought that as Jesus returned home to Nazareth, *He grew.* This is the third time in the first two chapters that Luke has referred to people growing. In 1:80 he informs us that John *"...grew and became strong in spirit..."* In 2:40 as we've highlighted already Luke confirms that the child Jesus *"...grew and became strong; He was filled with wisdom, and the grace of God was upon Him."* Finally, in 2:52 the same sort of theme is repeated. However, what is interesting is that in the previous two references, 1:80 and 2:40, Luke uses the same word for grew, namely, *auxánō* and the basic idea behind this word is that of increase, growing, enlarging that which lives already. The implication then is that both John and Jesus (though they grew in different ways), increased naturally and normally. When it comes to 2:52, Luke uses the word *prokóptō*, and carries with it the idea of not simply increase, but advancement. The word can mean to "beat forward", carrying with it the picture of cutting a path. Imagine coming to a field full of high grass and you had to get a machete out and cut out a pathway for yourself... that's the implication of the word. So what is Luke saying here? The growth he's now referring to is distinct and different from that mentioned before. I believe Luke is giving us an amazing key in the use of this one word. He's telling us that Jesus is cutting a growth path; that He didn't just grow, but that He grew intentionally or, put another way, *Jesus grew on purpose!* In 2:52, He's not merely growing naturally because He's healthy; rather He's advancing forward deliberately and growing on purpose!

I love what Andy Stanley said, "Everybody ends up somewhere in life. A few people end up somewhere on purpose."(12) Perhaps having asked and found the answers to the BIG questions, Jesus was able to return to the obscurity of Nazareth and live purposefully towards a higher call and a greater goal. Having tasted His Father's glory and stood in His Father's house, He was able to return to Galilee and set His sights on growing on purpose, deliberately, and intentionally advancing in the areas He knew would best prepare Him for His destiny. For the next eighteen years He deliberately grew in wisdom, strength and favour with God and with men and at thirty years old people suddenly wondered, "How did Jesus get so smart?" This one little word tucked away in this almost missable verse teaches us a life-transforming principle: that if we grow on purpose in the chrónos moments, we will be ready to go when the kairós opportunity arrives!

Study & Reflection

He excelled in the ordinary

Remind yourself of Luke 2:51. Did you grasp the significance in the difference between chronos time and kairos time?

Why is it important for an individual or local church to work through these ideas as they go forward?

How can a better understanding of chronos – process and kairos – event empower us to negotiate working out the will of God in our lives?

He embraced responsibility
Read again Mark 6:1-6. How is Jesus described?

If the people saw Jesus in the only way they knew how, in the context of His responsibilities, what does this tell us about Jesus' life before the beginning of His ministry at 30?

Look at the Andy Stanley quote. If you were God, what type of person would entrust eternal responsibility to?

He understood His destiny
Look at Luke 2:49. Why do people struggle with the idea that Jesus came to a place of understanding through His own learning or revelation as a man?

What passages of the Old Testament might have helped Jesus see who He was?

What are the BIG questions you are wrestling with right now and how have you sought to answer them? Let the Word of God guide you. Dig, digest and discern!

He grew deliberately
Read Luke 2:52. The idea behind the word translated grew is that of 'cutting a path'. If you were cutting a path from scratch, what might you need to think about, prepare for and do?

Are there any spiritual parallels from cutting a physical path to your growth in spirituality?

Stanley says, some people get to where they're going on purpose. Where are your actions and attitudes taking you?

Section 1:
Growing in Wisdom - IQ

2. How Did Jesus Get So Smart?

"And Jesus grew in wisdom..."

Over the years I've had the privilege of meeting some seriously smart people, so brilliant in their thinking that even with my two post graduate degrees, I felt like an intellectual ant standing beside them. I've read books filled with insights and thoughts framed with words and sentences that leave me gasping "wow"! Professor William Williams was one such person. He came to our Bible College to do some teaching during his sabbatical and, as he sat on his desk and opened the Bible to me as a second year Bible student, I concluded, "So that's what a Teacher looks like!" The Prof was fluent in biblical Hebrew, Greek and Aramaic and he was learning Egyptian as a pastime. This man had forgotten more stuff than I knew and he taught the Bible like he wrote it! However, he didn't just live in a library; during the term he taught us, he sat on the student common room floor with me, he shared meals with the students, we went on walks together where I largely listened while he talked. He took an interest in us and, as all authentic teachers should do, inspired us to learn. He had a brain the size of a continent, wrapped in a heart of humility and delivered knowledge with a passion to grow those around him. I met him for three months in 1985... that brief but glorious encounter lives on!

In my experience, there are different kinds of smart and I'm always a little saddened when we measure smart just one way, with a one-size-fits-all mentality. I have three children who are all smart, but in different ways, and how we measure them will determine who comes out the smartest! Too often our educational programmes aim for and recognise only one type of smart, which is good for those who fit, but not so good for those who don't.

I've come to realise and appreciate that there are different kinds of smart. There are "info-smart" people who know stuff; the sort of people you want on your phone-a-friend list on *Who Wants to be a Millionaire*, with sponge-like minds that absorb the type of information that would give Google a run for its money. There are "skill-smart" people who have understood what they are good at and maximize their particular talents to achieve something extraordinary. There are "purpose-smart" people, who have focused very much on their area of expertise and passion, and within that arena they really know what they know (but sometimes, beyond the boundary of their passion, the conversation quickly dies). Then there are "life-smart" people who have learned to make what they know work where they live. Regardless of the extent of their intellectual capability they can take what they know and make it work for them, or even if they don't know the details, they can still find a way to move forward. This is the sort of smart I am most impressed with and attracted to, for it's the ability to translate learning into life and move knowledge into how-to, incarnating what we know into how we live! This is at the heart of Bible wisdom: gaining knowledge for life's-sake, rather than knowledge for knowledge's-sake. Too many learn in order to know, when the Bible wants us to learn in order to grow. When my oldest daughter Elaina was learning to drive, I challenged her with a question: "Do you want to learn to pass a test or do you want to learn to drive?" When it comes to getting smart, we must not simply think knowledge, we must think life. Biblical wisdom teaches us this truth:

Nothing is taught until something is learned – nothing is learned until it is lived!

So how smart was Jesus?

Luke tells us He "...grew in wisdom...", but how could we tell? Of course, for many the answer is easy. Jesus was God in flesh, therefore His knowledge is boundless and therefore He's super-smart. I accept fully the *Godness* of Jesus and I believe He was fully God, the eternal Son of God poured into humanity. But Luke tells us He deliberately and intentionally grew in wisdom, which suggests (please don't stone me) there were things He didn't know and had to learn. His humanity had to learn without the aid of His deity and the evidence seems to suggest He did a pretty good job of growing in wisdom. Even a casual reading of the gospels demonstrates His cultural, intellectual, biblical and social wisdom. He knew His world, He knew stuff, He knew the Scriptures and He knew people because He learned about all of them. Let's look a little closer at how smart Jesus was.

Multi-lingual

From the evidence of His world and His work, I suggest that Jesus may have been able to speak at least four languages. We know as a Rabbi He was able to read, speak and write Hebrew, the language of the Tanakh. He's fluent in Aramaic, the language of the people and conducts most of His teaching through this medium. As a Jew growing up in Galilee (of the Gentiles), a region of Jewish enclaves surrounded by a large Gentile population, not far from the Decapolis, the ten cities, where Helenisation would still have had its influence, a working knowledge of Greek would have been advantageous in business when dealing with non-Jews. Perhaps too He had an understanding of Latin, the language of the Roman world who ruled Jesus' country at that time. As the leader of His home, a businessman and teacher, to be able to understand and speak Latin would have afforded Jesus a massive advantage. The multi-lingual context of His world is highlighted at the crucifixion of Jesus when Pilate ordered a sign to be fastened to His cross in three languages, Aramaic, Latin and Greek, reading "Jesus of Nazareth, the King of the Jews." (1) I submit to you, Jesus would have been able to read the sign in all three languages!

Craftsman

We traditionally think of Jesus as a carpenter, but the word *téktōn* implies that Jesus not only had a skill in wood, but perhaps in stone-masonry as well. Israel, even then, did not have an abundance of wood, so carpentry alone would have left Jesus vulnerable economically when the ability to expand and diversify ensured survival. Jesus could not have practised His trade in Nazareth alone, a tiny village, He would have had to work throughout the region, and without His own website to promote His skills, word of mouth was vital. If Jesus got work it was because He was good at what He did; known and recommended by many. Jesus was so good at what He did, that when His hometown labelled Him, they associated Him with His trade. When they refer to Him as "the carpenter" they're not putting Him down through this, but simply affirming that's what He does! Jesus learned how to make tools and use them so well that in an age where taxation was as much as 50%, where less than 5% of the population held all the wealth, where peasant subsistence was the norm, He was not only able to survive, but provide for His family. Jesus was "skill-smart".

Rabbi

When Jesus emerges as a 30-year-old man with an authority to teach, He's regarded by those who hear Him as a Rabbi, a term which literally meant "master" and would later come to signify "teacher". What's interesting is that in all the theological and doctrinal encounters that Jesus has with various sections of the religious community, they never question His scholarship. In fact, it could be argued they are so impressed by His scholarship they want to know "by what authority" He taught... or put another way, "Who taught You?" Jesus knew the Torah intimately, demonstrated so often not only in what He said, but what He left out. He rarely quoted a text; rather He taught truth. His knowledge of the Tanakh is so profound that even when confronted with seemingly unanswerable questions, He finds an answer. Jesus, an expert teacher, summarises the whole of the Law and the prophets (that's 39 books of the Old Testament or 24 books of the Tanakh) in two sentences... now that's smart!

In his book *Outliers*, Malcolm Gladwell identifies what he calls the 10,000-hour rule. He highlights that for those who are significantly successful in a particular area, they have all put in huge work in preparation and training to achieve their success... in most cases around 10,000 hours of preparation, which he describes as "...the magic number of greatness". He argues that achievement happens when three key things collide, namely:

Talent + Preparation + Opportunity = Achievement (2)

In a world that focuses on talent and craves opportunity, we should not forget the crucial role preparation plays. Without it, talent is wasted and opportunities are missed. So let's apply the 10,000-hour rule to Jesus as a Rabbi. Let's say that He starts to learn the Scriptures at the age of 5 and continues to study until He's 30 when His ministry begins. This means to become the "expert" in the Law that He was, He would have had to study the

Tanakh for approximately 400 hours per year, that's just over 7.69 hours per week. Wow!

As a leader I've been involved in helping in the training of leaders for many years. Often I ask leaders of churches and preachers how much time they devote to studying the Bible (often this is translated as studying for a sermon, which is not what I meant). The average tends to be around 2 hours per week. So if we applied the 10,000-hour rule to that scenario, it would take those leaders approximately 96 years to be called "master". Jesus was not only smart, but He worked hard at getting smart. When people heard Him teach they responded, "Wow, that's amazing… where did you get this stuff?" Answer: 25 years of continuous learning, while raising a family and serving a trade!

Storyteller

Jesus is famous for His story-telling ability, especially through what we call parables. In Sunday school I was taught that a parable was a "heavenly story with an earthly meaning", which is a pretty good definition as the word itself implies the idea of "side-by-side". Jesus' ability to teach through parables not only demonstrated His knowledge of biblical truth, but His insight into the world in which He lived, enabling Him to put the content of the Bible "side-by-side" with the context of His world. To do this well, Jesus needed an intimate knowledge of both.

A glance at just some of the side-by-side stories of Jesus (without looking at His wider teaching) shows how well He knew His world and those who lived in it. His illustrations were so attractive because they were so authentic.

Knowledge of agriculture
Parables of The Soils, The Wheat and Weeds, The Rich Fool, The Mustard Seed, The Yeast and The Growing Seed.

All of these were used in the Galilean section of His ministry, remembering that Galilee was a predominantly agricultural context.

Knowledge of finance

Parables of The Hidden Treasure, The Valuable Pearl, The Wasteful Manager, The Landowner and The Talents.

Knowledge of family

Parables of The Two Sons and The Ten Virgins.

Knowledge of ceremony

Parables about what defiles a person and about the places at the feast.

Knowledge of society

Parables of The Lost Sheep, The Lost Coin, The Lost Sons, The Rich Man and Lazarus, The Persistent Widow, The Good Samaritan, The Pharisee and the Tax Collector, The Wedding Banquet, The Unmerciful Servant, The House Owner, The Wise and Wicked Servants and The Bold Friend.

Through these everyday events and occurrences, Jesus illustrates the kingdom of God and biblical truth and the fact that He is able to do so not only shows His knowledge of the events but also the right context in which to use them. His more agricultural parables, for example, are used around Galilee, whereas His more apocalyptic parables around Jerusalem. He doesn't just know His world, but He knows what works best where. Now that's smart! Jesus is a great story-teller because He's able to connect truth to everyday life and He is an expert at doing this… because He knows both truth and life!

Friend

People liked Jesus because He liked people. He didn't talk down to people, He talked to them. He didn't just use them as illustrations,

He understood them and He didn't "people-watch", He lived with them! As we look at the spectacular 9% of the life of Jesus we see people at the heart of everything and we observe someone who is able to authentically connect to a wide range of individuals and groups. Jesus seems as comfortable with the poor as He does with the rich. He's able to engage with the religious experts and explain truth to a Gentile. He can eat with sinners and have supper with the elite, without suffering indigestion. He's as comfortable with one as He is with 5,000. Jesus learned how to handle people because Jesus learned about people. Jesus was "people-smart", and was so good with them we can read through the gospels without really noticing. It looks so natural because it is and He makes it look easy because He has worked so hard. One of the things I love about Jesus is that He refuses to be boxed in by the rules of the world He lives in. In His love for people and His desire to learn about them, He refuses to allow the traditionally accepted excuses to get in His way of being a friend to those around Him.

Jesus never used the personality excuse

I'm sure someone has or could do a personality profile of Jesus, but whatever shape His personality takes, He never once made who He was or how He was an excuse to reach out to people. Too many (and I've done it myself) excuse their lack of people-smartness because of their personality type with "Well, I'm not really a people person." I know what we mean by that, but that attitude soon becomes a wall preventing us from learning about those around us, thus allowing us to behave how we want.

Jesus never used the gender excuse

As a man He could have disengaged with women, especially in the culture of His day. Yet we see Jesus over and over again talking to women, connecting with women, teaching women, using women in a positive way in His teaching as examples of virtue and even having women as part of His discipleship group. In Luke's gospel alone there are twenty-seven cases in the text of the pairing of men and women where women are elevated on behalf of Jesus, in connection to Jesus or by Jesus Himself.(3)

Jesus never used the economic excuse

If Jesus reflected the context of Galilee, then life was economically hard. Some have suggested Jesus was poor, while others that He was a wealthy entrepreneur. Whatever His status, it would have been easy for Him to despise the rich and embrace the poor or despise the poor and embrace the rich... yet He does neither. Nowhere do we see Jesus shunning the wealthy for the sake of their wealth alone. He offers the kingdom to the poor, but He does not bar the rich. Much is made of the fact that Luke demonstrates Jesus eating with sinners on at least five occasions, but we should not ignore the fact that He also eats with the religious elite, many of them wealthy, on at least three occasions in the same gospel.

Jesus never used the ethnic excuse

As a good Jew He would have been encouraged to stick to His own kind, yet we see Him not only engaging with non-Jews, but He seems extremely comfortable with them. Though Matthew tells us His ministry was primarily to the "lost sheep of the house of Israel", this does not prevent Him from connecting to Romans, Greeks, Syrians and Samaritans. Ethnicity is an excuse only for those who refuse to learn.

Jesus never used the geographic excuse

In the world Jesus lived in there was animosity between the North and the South. The South represented purity, the heartland of faith, the residence of the Temple, whereas the North was detached, diverse and unattractive. "Nazareth... where's that?" "Galilee... what good can come from there?" Though Jesus spends a significant time ministering in His native Galilean context, He doesn't allow this to form a barrier to others. When He ministers in the South and in the City of Jerusalem, there's no angst because His focus is not a place… but people.

Jesus never used the religious excuse

Though Jesus came to fulfil the Law and did so completely, He never allowed religion to stand in the way of connecting people to God. When so many in His day urged separation, Jesus developed a reputation for being a glutton and a drunk (though this slur was not true). We tend to think that the Pharisees followed Jesus around to criticise and irritate Him, but maybe they saw Him as a good Pharisee gone bad (His theology was closest to that of the Pharisees) and they were trying to save Him. Jesus, this charismatic Pharisee, refused to separate from people because it was for the people He came, even the unholy, sinful ones. He touched the leper, ate with sinners, drank from the well of Samaritans, healed Gentiles and complimented Romans, all without compromising His spirituality or the integrity of the Law.

Jesus was attractive because He was authentic. His authenticity not only made Him attractive, but granted Him a moral authority with the people that ensured record-breaking audiences most places He went. Jesus refused to hide behind excuses but instead gave Himself to living with, learning about and loving the people around Him.

Jesus was smart… but He wasn't smart because He was God. He was smart because He learned. He grew on purpose in the areas that would make Him smart and thus make Him ready for His ministry. As we look at Him, we observe He was smart culturally, intellectually, biblically, economically and socially. Not bad for a peasant from the north! Jesus demonstrates to us that if we determine to grow, we will, and if we are intentional about learning the right things, in the right places from the right people, we too will get smart!

Study & Reflection

"And Jesus grew in wisdom..."

The Bible encourages us to be life-smart, to take the knowledge we've acquired and make it work. Consider this statement: "Nothing is taught until something is learned. Nothing is learned until something is lived."

What does this mean and what are the implications to how we learn and live?

Do you think of Jesus as life-smart or have you put His ability down to the fact that He is God?

If we incorporate family responsibilities, job demands and Bible study (as a rabbi in learning), what challenges would Jesus have faced as He grew in wisdom?

Growth in life-smart wisdom is a continuous process. What are the biggest challenges you face in making wisdom growth an essential and continuous part of your life and how can they be addressed and overcome?

3. Life-long Learner

"And Jesus grew in wisdom..."

I love the idea of life-long learning. I've learnt more since I left school than when I was there. I've learnt more about life, theology and ministry since leaving Bible College than I did whilst studying there. I'm not saying that in any way to discredit my education, because I'm deeply grateful for it and really enjoyed it. But I left school at 16 and left Bible College at 20. I've lived a whole lot since then and learned to learn on the journey. I have embraced the fact that learning is not an activity, something I do, rather it is a lifestyle, someone I am.

This sits comfortably with the ideas that Jesus would have engaged with in 1st century Judaism and in the world of the New Testament church. Rabbi's would take *talmidim* – students who would dedicate their lives to the Rabbi, his lifestyle and his teaching, taking on his yoke and learning from him. This idea is also captured in the term disciple, *mathētēs*, which has at its heart the picture of a learner. In fact, the root of the word indicates the idea of thought accompanied by action or endeavour. Disciples were intentional learners, dedicated to their teacher or mentor. Their lives were apprenticed to the master and their ambition was to learn from him as much as possible. In calling His would-be disciples Jesus promised, *"Come follow Me and I will **make** you..."*(1)

But how would a *talmid* or *mathētēs* be made?

Take My yoke upon you and learn from Me, for I am gentle and humble in heart, and you will find rest for your souls. For My yoke is easy and My burden is light.(2)

Jesus didn't call His followers to a meeting or a Bible study programme, rather He called them to a life of learning. I always get a little uneasy at the idea of a "discipleship course". I know we all have them, and of course I'm in no way against them, as long as we don't create the idea that the 5-week course is all someone has to learn to engage with all God has. Any discipleship course should not only inform, but also provoke. Our ambition must be that by the end of the course the disciples want more and begin the journey of getting God-smart, a journey that will last until the day they die!

Life-long learning is at heart an attitude which creates an aptitude, which in turn produces actions. It moves from a good idea to a belief system expressed in a lifestyle. It needs to become in us all a "first-nature" feature.

Smart people understand they don't have all the answers!

"The self taught man seldom knows anything accurately, and he does not know a tenth as much as he could have known if he had worked under teachers, and besides, he brags, and is the means of fooling other thoughtless people into going and doing as he himself has done."(3)

Arrogance is simply a reflection of our ignorance.

Smart people understand that learning is a fundamental requirement for success!

"It is the capacity to develop and improve their skills that distinguishes leaders from their followers… the goal each day must be to get a little better, to build on the previous day's progress."(4)

The only place where success appears before work is in the dictionary!

Smart people understand that learning isn't a one-off experience!

School is not a place, it's a process and the sooner we learn this, the less fractious life can become. With this mindset, every day becomes an opportunity to learn from something or someone and humility paves the way for smart living.

Questions are a sign you're smart, not stupid!

Smart people understand that no one is born smart; they get smart!

The story is told of a tourist who, whilst visiting some historic villages, asked a resident:

"Were there any famous people born in this village?"

To which the resident replied,

"No, only babies!"

How we live is more important than where we were born!

So how can we get smart and how can life-long learning become a reality for us?

Take a moment to read Proverbs 4:1-9.

Within this passage lies some of the secrets of getting **S.M.A.R.T.**

S-eek out smart people

Listen, my sons, to a father's instruction... (v1)

The gaining of wisdom and understanding is set in the context of a relationship, in this instance, that of a father with his sons, thus immediately putting learning in the arena of life. The sons were called to learn from a person who was not merely talking about wisdom, but practising it in front of them. As a parent of three children I have learned, if my instruction doesn't match my lifestyle – if there is a disconnection between what I say and what I do – my children will soon point that out. If my instruction to my children is to mean anything, it must be carried on the credibility of a life lived wisely. The father in this passage isn't just clever, he's smart. He doesn't just know truth, he's living wisdom. He's embraced her in the same way he's calling his sons to, that's why he can teach them with such confidence.

I give you sound learning... (v2)

Twice in the passage the father uses the expression,

...do not forsake... (vs 2 & 6)

Literally the idea here is "don't loose the bonds", stay connected to the truth I'm teaching and with that, stay connected to me. Wisdom is connected to people as well as to truth!

A young boy once approached his father to ask,

"Dad, why does the wind blow?"

"I don't know, son."

"Dad, where do the clouds come from?"

"I'm not sure son."

"Dad, what makes a rainbow?"

"No idea, son."

"Dad, do you mind me asking you all these questions?"

"Not at all, son. How else are you going to learn?"(5)

If we're going to ask questions and if we're going to life-learn, then we need to seek out and spend time with smart people. This will cost time, effort and money, but if we're smart we'll do it. A few months ago I was visited by a former Bible student from the college where I occasionally teach. He made a powerful confession to me as we sat in my church office. "I wish I had paid more attention to the teachers, not just what they taught." Having left college, he realized, a little too late, that smart people are as important as smart facts. Though a good student, he wished he had been a better *talmid*!

Aside from Almighty God,(6) what smart people are in your world? What areas of your life need the input of smart people? I encourage you to identify and connect, because smart people love spending time with people who want to get smart!

M-ake time to learn

Four times the word "get" is used in this passage, twice in verse 5 and twice in verse 7. Each time the word is the same, carrying with it the idea of buying or purchasing. The getting here is both intentional and expensive, but in the context of what is being purchased, the learner deems the cost a bargain! We'll come back to verse 7 later in this chapter, but verse 5 says, *"Get wisdom, get understanding; do not forget my words or swerve from them."*

In order to get something we must make it a priority at some level, whether that be energy, time or finance. Getting requires focus, intention and determination. Getting will mean invariably the prioritization of one thing at the expense of another. Aside from money, time is one of the most precious commodities we have, but unlike money, once time is gone, there's no way to get it back. Smart people make time to learn, not simply in a formal sense, but throughout the shape of their lives: time to read, time to listen, time to talk, time to think and time to change.

Lots of people want to be smart as long as it can be packaged in a nice little "fast-food" box and they can get it to go. But unlike fast-food, learning requires preparation, it's not meant to be digested alone, it lasts more than five minutes and it's good for us! Some things just can't be rushed and getting smart is one of those things. We never know when or from whom or what we're going to learn, but we cannot reduce learning to an event – it needs to be part of an experience; different aspects of a multi-course meal.

In his book *Courageous Leadership*, Bill Hybels speaks of the 360 degree leader: one who can lead south – leading those under us, something he calls "...a leader's first instinct". One who can lead north – leading those over us, and one who can also lead east/west, influencing peer-group settings.

But what about leading "inwardly"? Quoting Dee Hock's work *The Art of Chaordic Leadership* he concludes, "It is management of self that should occupy 50 percent of our time and the best of our ability. And when we do that the ethical, moral and spiritual elements of management are inescapable."(7)

Nelson in his book *Spirituality and Leadership* concurs:

"...the most effective leaders invest significant time and energy making sure the 'axe is sharp' – that they are well read and that their mind, body and soul are at their best. When the inner leader becomes depleted, it adversely affects everything the leader touches. When the inner leader is nourished, the entire organization benefits."(8)

The idea, for most of us, that we could block out 50% of our week or month for "self-leadership" or personal development would be an impossibility, unless of course we're prepared to weave such learning into the fabric of our lives, part of the everyday, the ordinary and the routine. This level of intention forces us to look at who is in our lives – and how we might learn with them? It causes us to ask, what opportunities are available to me right now and how can I more effectively engage with them? It challenges us to consider what changes might need to take place in our lives and how we can be more creative in our context. As someone once said, "Necessity is the mother of invention."

We usually don't find a way until we have to, or want to.

"Wisdom is the greatest possession anyone can have, and the young man should make winning her the primary goal of his life." (9) Such a goal will cost... and it will cost us in time!

A-pply what you learn

Do not forsake wisdom, and she will protect you; love her, and she will watch over you. (v6)

I like how the Message puts it:

Don't deviate an inch! Never walk away from Wisdom – she guards your life…

Again the idea here is of fully engaging with wisdom, not merely at an intellectual level, but with our hearts and lifestyle. The true proof that we have embraced wisdom is that we live wise. We touched on this in chapter 2, but it's worth a little reminder here:

Nothing is truly taught until something is learned
Nothing is truly learned until it is lived

In the context of this passage and biblical thought, lifestyle is a reflection of belief system. Our beliefs are not merely understood in terms of confession, but via the vehicle of conduct. In other words, what we do is what we believe. This is how the sons are being tutored so that their knowing would be expressed in their living.

The actions of Jesus the night He washed their feet must have truly blown the minds of His young disciples. He left His place of honour as Rabbi, and assumed the mantle and duties of servant, washing the feet of His friends. When He returned to His place He asked,

*"Do you **understand** what I have **done** for you?"*

In other words, "Have you learned something tonight?" But note how He taught them, through His actions.

Before they have the chance to answer, Jesus drives the lesson home: *"You call Me 'Teacher' and 'Lord,' and rightly so, for that is what I am. Now that I, your Lord and Teacher, have washed your feet, you also **should wash** one another's feet. I have set you an example that **you should do** as I have done for you. I tell you the truth, no servant is greater than his master, nor is a messenger* *greater than the one who sent him. Now that you know these things, you will be blessed **if you do them**.*"(10)

Whatever lesson Jesus wanted them to learn, the evidence that they had learned it would be seen not in their sermons and clever theses, but in their actions. If they could authentically wash the feet of those around them, this would be the sign that something had been taught… because it was being lived. Failure to apply the learning and to wash feet would demonstrate that although they had just witnessed one of the most amazing teaching-actions in the whole life of Jesus, they had learned nothing!

I remember the day my oldest daughter Elaina passed her driving test. She managed it at her first attempt, trumping her dad by one! When she got home she was so excited, in fact she broke the news to me over the phone resulting in partial deafness in my right ear. That evening our church had worship practice at the church centre and both Elaina and Simeon were involved and Beth-Anne our youngest was due at a dance class. Over dinner Elaina suggested that she could take Beth-Anne to her dance class on the way to worship practice with Simeon. At that moment I heard my mouth say, "Yes, that will be great," and then secretly started to worry about what I'd just agreed to. As I watched Elaina leave the drive way and proceed up the road I was struck by the thought that my three most precious possessions were all in the same car being driven by someone on their first journey without supervision! This was the moment of truth. This was the moment when I'd find out if her instruction had become learning! She not only made it home, but has clocked a whack of miles ever since. When we "do" it's a sign we've learned!

R-esource yourself

Wisdom is supreme; therefore get wisdom. Though it cost you all you have, get understanding. (v7)

There is a degree of disagreement over the translation of this verse and due to certain ambiguity some have suggested it should read: "The beginning of wisdom is, Get Wisdom!" The Message phrases it, "Above all and before all, do this: Get Wisdom! Write this on the top of your list."

I like the idea that the beginning of wisdom is the decision to get wisdom. It makes sense and fits with the rest of the book. For some people the wisest thing they decided to do was to go after wisdom. But as we've seen already from verse 5, going after wisdom costs and it may even cost us financially. Meeting up with a smart person costs (by the way, if they are giving you their time, you should at least pick up the coffee bill or pay for the meal!) Buying books costs. Going to a seminar, costs. Saying no to self costs. Getting a degree costs. As I write this chapter I'm thinking of 4 students who are currently on a Masters in Missional Leadership course, on which I teach. Two of them travel from Holland, one from the USA and one from South Africa – and they do it five weekends a year for two years! That's a cost! Everything of value is worth paying for and wisdom, learning, getting smart is no exception. We can't get smart on the cheap. We won't get to learn from smart people by cutting costs. When it comes to wisdom there will never be a pay off, until we are prepared to pay out.

Though there are still exceptions in some parts of the world, for many of us we are resource rich. Books, podcasts, dvds, learning opportunities and connecting possibilities abound as never before. In some cases the choice is bewildering and part of being smart is knowing what to pick and what to leave. This is why I get frustrated at those who miss the opportunities to get smart on the basis that there's nothing for them, or that they are too busy to engage. If we want to, we can. It's that simple. I know someone is going to get annoyed at me and suggest I don't know what I'm talking about. But if I've learned anything from smart people, they will do anything (provided it's moral and legal) to grow and develop. The key issue is settling what we want, then we make a plan to resource ourselves empowering us to grow.

What are you willing to pay to get smart? The price will probably determine the prize!

T-ake your opportunities

Esteem her, and she will exalt you; embrace her, and she will honour you. (v8)

I love the picture contained within this verse that if we will esteem wisdom, "lift up and elevate her", she'll make us "tall".

Listen, my son, accept what I say, and the years of your life will be many. (v10)

This discourse concludes with the same appeal with which he started: "Listen". In other words, take the opportunities that are now being afforded to you, don't ignore them or take them for granted, but right now, grasp them, embrace them, take hold of wisdom, be intentional about elevating her in your life, and she will make you walk tall and journey straight!

Over the years I've sat with people who have come to me and asked, "Will you mentor me? I want to learn from what you have." Now I love this approach, but I'm also conscious that like diet plans and New Year's resolutions, people can be excited at the beginning of the journey but soon lose enthusiasm.

So I usually ask two questions:

What is it you want?

What do you think I can teach you?

There's no right answer, but I want to hear their hearts.

At the end of the first session I usually set them a task, relevant to where I think they are. I don't set another appointment; I leave it to them to "chase me". I'm available, but they must want me. I know it sounds pretentious, but it's truly not. However, it is amazing how often that one task is enough to sift out those who think they want to be mentored, from those who really do want to be mentored. Many like the idea of meeting, of being mentored by a master, but few are willing to consistently take the opportunities, make the call, set up the appointments, pay for lunch and go all the way.

We see this in various moments in the life of Jesus:

"Follow Me!"

"Lord, first let me go and bury my father."

"I will follow You, Lord; but first let me go back and say goodbye to my family."(11)

Opportunities come and go, but smart people take more than they miss!

Jesus got smart on purpose and so can we! It's not easy, because it requires both intention and investment, but the pay-off for the pay-out is more than we can imagine.

She will set a garland of grace on your head and present you with a crown of splendour. (v9)

Jesus grew in wisdom… so can you!

Life-long learning – now that's S.M.A.R.T.

Study & Reflection

"And Jesus grew in wisdom…"

Read Proverbs 4:1-9. In the light of the idea of *talmidim* and *mathētēs* how might you understand the statement, "learning is not an activity, something I do, rather it is a lifestyle, someone I am."

In what areas of your life would you love to grow in wisdom?

Seek out smart people
Think of the following areas as an example (or you can pick your own, if need-related): Money, marriage, parenting and authentic faith.

Now, for each area list at least 2 smart people who's "yoke" you might learn from. Is it worth an approach to them?

Make time to learn
If getting wisdom was the primary goal, how intentional are you to learn? To what extent do you let wisdom happen (learning from the stuff of life) and how much do you make happen?

Apply what you learn
Don't leave wisdom in your head, get it into your life.

What practicalities can help us apply wisdom?

What factors can indicate we're applying the wisdom we're learning?

Resource yourself
Everything of worth costs. Is wisdom-growth worth investing in? Looking at the areas where you'd like to or need to grow in wisdom, what resources (people, books, classes etc) are available to you within your sphere of movement and influence?

What are you prepared to pay to get that wisdom?

Take your opportunities
Have you any regrets of wisdom-growth opportunities you missed?
What opportunities to learn and grow are available to you?

If in the next 12 months you identified one area of growth, what would it be… and is there an opportunity for you to be taught and grow in that area?

Section 2:
Growing in Stature - PQ

4. Strong for the Journey

"And Jesus grew in stature..."

Growing up in Belfast as a child of the Troubles, I lived with a tension when it came to my understanding of Jesus. The Jesus I read about in the gospels inspired me, challenged me and seemed like a properly testosterone filled man. But in Sunday school, children's clubs and the media, Jesus was often portrayed as wispy, weak, much too good looking for any one man, with His flowing blonde hair, milky pimple-less skin and of course those eyes; stunning, penetrating blue eyes. The Jesus of the gospels seemed to be all man, but the Jesus of my story books and flash cards seemed, how can I put this, very comfortable with His "feminine side"! As I child I can remember watching with eager expectation the movie *The Greatest Story Ever Told*. It seemed to last forever, telling the story of Jesus from birth to resurrection. I watched the same movie as a teenager and wondered how I'd managed to sit through it first time. Jesus (portrayed by actor Max von Sydow) represented a Jesus I struggled to take seriously, with his soft hands and spotlessly clean white robe. He spoke like he'd been to seminary and seemed disconnected from the ordinary people around him. In truth, I'd struggle to follow this Jesus to the end of my street, let alone the end of the world!

In our reverence for Jesus we've been in danger of stripping away His humanity. Though God is *Other*, if we apply this too zealously to the incarnation, we can cause the human-ness of Jesus to lose credibility and with it, reality! It's a tricky tension to manage, but one we must grasp. For some Christians, the thought that Jesus was tired, got a blister, was hungry, or needed to go the toilet, is too much information. Yet, when understood properly, rather than diminish Him, it enhances His manhood and His message.

In 2011 the BBC ran a series of four programmes on the final days of Jesus called, *The Passion*. As with any depiction of the life of Jesus there was much controversy and dispute. However, one of the disturbing factors the series threw up was how the ordinariness of Jesus was presented, even showing Jesus with dirt under His finger nails…! The truth is that Jesus was fully human in a tough and uncompromising world, and to survive, He needed to be strong.

Luke tells us that Jesus *"grew… in stature…"*. I like how The Message puts it: *"Jesus matured, growing up in both body and spirit…"*. The primary idea behind the word used here, *hēlikía*, is of "coming of age", in this context, the sense of physical maturity. Again we can slide into thinking that this is purely down to natural development; provided Jesus is healthy He's going to mature physically. But understood in the context of deliberate or intentional growth and coupled to the fact that all the areas mentioned (namely wisdom, God and men) in fact represent an overall maturation of Jesus, I do not think I'm stretching the point too far by suggesting that Jesus considered His physical development in a deliberate and intentional way. Of course, I'm not suggesting Jesus was a fitness freak, a member of the local gym or a regular participant in the Jerusalem marathon, but I am confident, in light of the type of ministry He was being called to fulfil, He would have taken His health and well-being seriously, taking responsibility for His physicality.

Just a little glimpse at the 9% shows a Jesus who was strong… and here are some clues that show us how.

His world

Some scholars have suggested that life expectancy in the world of Jesus was around 30 years of age. A combination of the general harshness of life, meagre diet, disease and political uncertainty, all made an early demise a strong possibility. Luke's gospel shows Jesus on at least eight occasions eating with both sinners and the religious and one gets the impression that food was in abundance and life was good. However, recent research has brought to light some startling suggestions. Most people lived a predominantly vegetarian diet with meat being an occasional luxury. Even though, for example, the Galilean region had an abundance of fish, during the days of Jesus, Galilee was deemed a "royal lake" and the fish caught there suffered heavy taxation. Life was tough and during famine or more lean seasons, one might hear the phrase, "While the fat person becomes lean, the lean person becomes dead." Most people in Jesus' world, including Jesus, lived lean… life was never easy, at any time!(1) Jesus was strong!

His job

As I've hinted already, Jesus was probably a *téktōn*, someone who had skills not only in carpentry, but stone masonry and other essential building skills. For Jesus to specialise only in wood in a country that built most things out of stone, would have left Him economically vulnerable. Even today, with health and safety codes, proper breaks and holidays, anyone who works in the building trade will tell you it's hard work. Back in the days of Jesus, if one didn't work, one didn't eat! Many of the beggars on the streets of Jerusalem were there because of sickness, disability and injury, which left them incapacitated and unable to work. Unless someone had a strong and generous family network around them, the prospects of being unemployable were disastrous in the 1st century world. Dealing with trees and stone every day meant Jesus had to be healthy and strong. His health was the key to His wealth. Jesus would have had strong hands and a muscular physique, legs that could withstand long walks, being able to scale new buildings and stand for long hours in the middle-eastern heat. Jesus was strong!

His journeys

Though the Israel of Jesus' world was relatively small, north-south 150 miles, east to west around 70 miles, nonetheless it is important for us to remember that for most people, probably including Jesus, the main mode of transport was walking. I've been to Israel twice and both times managed to travel around in luxurious air-conditioned comfort. Not so for Jesus. Even the simplest journey required planning and time. Until Jesus started His ministry He lived in Nazareth. His home village was situated in a high valley among the most southern limestone hills on the Lebanon range; 1500m above sea level; the base of the valley was 370m above sea level. Steep hills rise up to the north and east sides, while on the west side they reach up to 500m… so, just getting to Nazareth was a hike. In fact, from Capernaum to Nazareth it was uphill all the way. Capernaum, the home village of Peter, was more than likely the Galilean headquarters for Jesus' ministry and when we read that Jesus went from Nazareth *down* to Capernaum,(2) depending on how direct the route, this was a walk of approximately 20 miles. Some other distances around Galilee you might recognize are: Nazareth to Cana (about 12 miles), Cana to Capernaum (18 miles) and Capernaum to Bethsaida (approx. 12 miles). We hear of Jesus going down to Jerusalem, and depending on His starting point in Galilee, this was a journey of around 120 miles, that's a 240 mile round trip back to His home. Jesus goes up to Caesarea Philippi (where we hear Peter's confession) and to Mt. Hermon (the traditional site of the transfiguration) covering about 50 miles. In another trip north, Jesus leaves from Capernaum and goes up into Phoenicia to the cities of Tyre and Sidon. He then returns south, journeys around the Sea of Galilee and into the area of Decapolis (the ten cities) from there north again to Capernaum. Without being sure of exactly how Jesus travelled, a calculated guesstimate of this journey is around 250 miles... on foot!

I think you get the picture. It's easy to read a text quickly and move on. What has cost us only a few seconds of time may have taken Jesus more than a day. Those few words disguise the fact that Jesus was strong enough to make those journeys and engage with His world in that way. Imagine that instead of driving the 3 or 4 miles to church this Sunday, which normally takes you about 10 minutes, you had to walk it. Think of the time you would have to give and think of the energy it would cost you. This was the reality of Jesus' world. Jesus was strong!

His fast

In the summer of 1997 I engaged on one of the toughest challenges of my life, a 40-day fast. I felt strongly that God led me to do this and it coincided with my leaving my first church and taking up a new post in Rotherham. With the help of my wife Dawn, we made all the necessary preparations, including a medical from my doctor... a very interesting conversation. On the first day of the fast I can remember thinking, "I'm doing this for the next month and a half." Over the forty days I lost over 3 stones, but yet, by the end wasn't that hungry. In fact, not eating in itself was the least of my challenges. The big struggles were *social* – it's amazing how much of life revolves around food; *psychological* – keeping my mind off food wasn't easy, especially when I closed my eyes and saw flying hamburgers; *sexual* – I missed the physical intimacy of being with my wife; *physical* – I had to conserve energy while trying to carry on with the normal stuff of life; and, of course, *spiritual* – seeking God, listening for answers, engaging in warfare that pushed me to my limit... all of these areas were more pressing to me than not having food. When I eventually broke my fast, it took me over a month to get back to anything like normal eating habits and in some ways that was worse than the fast.

Look at how the Bible describes Jesus' fast:

Jesus, full of the Holy Spirit, returned from the Jordan and was led by the Spirit in the desert, where for forty days he was tempted by the devil. He ate nothing during those days, and at the end of them He was hungry... Jesus returned to Galilee in the power of the Spirit...(3)

When read quickly, we miss some powerful things;

He's not eating for forty days, that's almost six weeks in real money.

He's fasting in the desert. I've been to the area where it's thought Jesus spent His time during the fast. The terrain is barren and unforgiving, hot during the day and cold during the night... extreme.

Throughout the forty days *He's being tempted.* The gospels highlight only three temptations, but clearly there were more, and I would suggest the temptations Jesus endured covered every area of human life and experience.

He's alone. Mark tells us that He was with *"...wild animals, and angels attended Him"*(4), but as far as human company is concerned, Jesus went through this on His own.

Then it simply says, *"Jesus returned...".* Clearly some level of recovery time would have been needed, but the fact that Jesus is able to come out of such an ordeal and relatively quickly engage in ministry, says something of His spiritual, psychological and physical strength.

Over the years I've heard people with their bellies hanging over their belts criticise Jesus for being weak – the same people who think their world is falling apart because their main course is a little late. Jesus was no wimp! If we have the courage to look we can see that Jesus had to have been in great shape going into the fast in order to survive the rigours of the fast. Jesus was strong!

His death

Numerous words have been written on the horror and brutality of Jesus' death. However, suffice to say, Jesus endured a traumatic physical ordeal, beginning with Gethsemane and including His death, which lasted without respite somewhere in the region of sixteen hours. In between Gethsemane (which means olive press) where Luke tells us *"...His sweat was like drops of blood falling to the ground"*(5), to the moment He cried, *"It is finished"*(6), at the end of six hours on the cross, Jesus was beaten, punched, deprived of sleep, whipped and interrogated by the Sanhedrin, Herod and Pilate. During this process He crosses the city of Jerusalem a number of times. The night begins in the upper room somewhere near the southwest quarter. From there He and His disciples head northeast to Gethsemane just outside the city walls, in sight of the Temple. From Gethsemane He's taken down the Kidron Valley, parallel to the city wall, in through the Ashpot or Tekoa Gate to the palace of the High Priest in the south of the city. From Caiaphas He's off to Pilate's judgment hall at the far north of the city, close to the temple mount. Pilate then sends Him to Herod, residing at the west of the city in his royal palace. From Herod it's back again to Pilate and then from Pilate, it's northwest out of the city with His cross to the place of execution. Jesus is then nailed to the cross and after six hours, John tells us,

With that, He bowed His head and gave up His spirit.(7)

Even here, John hints strongly that Jesus' life was not taken, but was given. It's as if Jesus chooses the moment of His death.

Can you see the strength of Jesus in all this? He is dragged from pillar to post, harassed, abused, tortured, interrogated and eventually crucified. But in it all, He's standing with dignity and heroic resolve. Jesus was strong!

I've highlighted these areas to show how physically strong Jesus actually was and to demonstrate that as Luke suggests, "Jesus grew in stature"; Jesus was fit for purpose! Too often in pursuit of "spiritual ministry" we neglect the physical, yet from the life of Jesus we realise that the spiritual in some ways would not have been possible if Jesus had not been physically strong. This, of course, does not mean that everyone who aspires to spiritual ministry has to be physically fit, for there are many who do amazing things for God in and through great physical restriction and disability. However, what I am seeking to demonstrate is this: knowing that His ministry might involve great physical demands, it stands to reason that Jesus prepared for this, by ensuring He was physically prepared and ready.

If you wanted to run in the London Marathon next year, it would be foolish to just turn up and run. I'm not saying you couldn't do it, but I'm pretty certain you could do it better if you took your preparation seriously. Out goes grease-filled fried breakfasts, in comes a healthy diet regime. Out goes lazy nights watching your favourite DVD box set, in comes regular runs that get longer and longer the closer you get to the event. The more you prepare, theoretically at least, the better you'll run. Very few of us would dream of running 26 miles 385 yards without giving serious intention to some physical preparation, yet so many look at their life-purpose and almost entirely neglect any consideration of growing in stature and issues of health and well-being. Our purpose might not look like Jesus', but it will put demands upon us that will require physical strength and resolve. We must not allow our physicality to eclipse our spirituality, as happens in so much of our shallow western culture, but neither must we ignore the link between the physical and the spiritual when it comes to our purpose, ministry and dreams.

I do not know what tomorrow holds, but if there are no terrible shocks, sicknesses or debilitating experiences, then I want to be as well prepared as possible for the purpose for which God has called me. I want to live "fit for purpose". I want to have the strength to run and stand and I want to have the same confession as Caleb, who at 85 years old, 45 years after he first caught sight of the land of promise, declared,

I am still as strong today as the day Moses sent me out; I'm just as vigorous to go out to battle now as I was then.(8)

During the 9% of Jesus' life, what we refer to as His public ministry, Jesus was able to travel the length and breadth of the land and engage in a rigorous ministry that touched many lives. He demonstrates that rather than being a wimpish figure, floating around 1st century Israel, He is strong, dynamic and determined. Luke tells us that Jesus grew in stature, and in those silent years He prepared Himself so well that He was fit for purpose and He was able to finish that which God had given Him to do.

Through His example He calls to us all – get fit for purpose!

Study & Reflection

"And Jesus grew in stature..."

If you were to describe Jesus from the pictures, paintings, movies and sermons you've experienced, what would He look like?

Why do you think so many might think of Jesus as weak, whispy or effeminate?

In what ways do you appreciate and even admire the strength of Jesus, having read the chapter, that perhaps you didn't before?

Why is that?

Having read the chapter and looked afresh at the gospels, how would you describe Jesus now?

5. The Spirituality of Physicality

"And Jesus grew in stature..."

Throughout my teenage years attending a Pentecostal church, I was aware of the tension that existed between the spiritual and the physical. These arenas of my life were seen as two separate segments and, to my memory, never discussed in any interconnected or integrated way. The only time we addressed the physical was in the context of need (someone needed to be healed, for instance) or in the context of sin, where the "flesh" was seen as an enemy to our spirituality. Being schooled in the King James Version of the Bible, the concept of human nature or selfish ambition was understood in the realm of *flesh*, creating the impression for a young Christian that anything relating to my flesh was something wrong, or at war with the "spiritual man" within. As a young man active in numerous sports, including running, football and judo, I was often reminded of the words of Scripture (for authenticity quoted in the KJV):

For bodily exercise profiteth little: but godliness is profitable unto all things, having promise of the life that now is, and of what is to come.(1)

These words added to my tension in two ways. Firstly, they suggested to me that my physical exercise and spiritual development were somehow in opposition to one another. Though I had no objection to the superiority of godliness over bodily exercise, the subtle nuance I picked up was that these two aspects of my life were in no way connected. Secondly, any physical exercise was seen as a distraction from my pursuit of godliness, and therefore although there was some value in it, I shouldn't pay too much attention to it. The result was that while engaged in any sport or physical training, I wrestled with a measure of guilt and, at best, a sense of futility. Better to pray than run; better to study the Bible than develop my body!

Of course, Paul wasn't telling Timothy not to take care of himself. Rather, he placed the obsession with physicality within the Roman world in the context of that which is most important. Paul wasn't saying physical development is bad or without value; nor was he separating it from our view of spirituality; rather he was asking Timothy to ensure that his spirituality drove the physical aspect of his life, not the other way around.

For physical training is of some value, but godliness has value for all things… (NIV)

The Message puts it:

Exercise daily in God – no spiritual flabbiness, please! Workouts in the gymnasium are useful, but a disciplined life in God is far more so!

As we saw in the previous chapter, Jesus was strong! He could not have achieved everything that was asked of Him without paying attention to His physical development and wellbeing. So if Jesus grew in stature and physical maturity, how can we? To help me, and hopefully encourage you, I've developed an acrostic around the word S.T.R.O.N.G:

S-pirituality includes physicality

Though we must recognise that we are spiritual beings in a physical/material world, we also must accept that the physical carries the spiritual. The Scriptures describe our bodies as "temples of the Holy Spirit"(2) crafting the picture for us of the individual and gathered community forming a "body" or house in which the Holy Spirit can dwell, and through which He can work.

By implication, the temple, house or body is important and it must be the responsibility of the individual or community to look after it in such a way that it is "fit for purpose". Many, of course, read *fit for purpose* only in spiritual terms. In other words, a good temple for the Spirit to dwell in is clean, holy and pure. Though I totally agree, I want to add another important aspect: that of ensuring (as much as we possibly can) that the physical wellbeing of our body reflects the worship we give to the God who dwells within. Many Christian communities have sacrificed to build and maintain a physical building for God to live in, arguing that the quality and excellence of the facility is in direct relation to the greatness of the God they serve. If this principle can be applied to a building (even though the Bible tells us God doesn't live in buildings), how much more should it be applied to our bodies, when the Bible tells us that *this* is where God lives!

Today, I view the directive from Paul to Timothy in 1 Timothy 4:8 very differently from how I understood it as a teenager. I realise that physical training and workouts are not only useful, but necessary for the purpose to which I believe I am called. I no longer see physical development as an add-on that serves my spirituality, I see my physicality as part of my spirituality. Placed in the big picture of my life purpose in service to God, this understanding has changed everything I do. So now, when I rest, when I run, when I play squash, I see this as an aspect of my spiritual growth through the physical realm. Executed with a right vision and proper motive, physical exercise is as spiritual an act as prayer or Bible study. They are not in competition, rather they flow together as complementary elements of the whole.

Speaking of the holistic nature of true biblical spirituality, Nelson puts it brilliantly when he concludes:

"We need to intersect our work, home, community and sexuality with God ... we must intermix the realms. Whatever God touches becomes sacred. Spirituality that isn't 24/7 is just hollow religion – a segregated component of a non-integrated person."(3)

For many, physicality serves spirituality, but how might our behaviour change if we decide that spirituality *includes* physicality?

T-rain on purpose, for purpose

For a few years I have been a member of a local gym, and over that period I've seen a pattern emerge in gym membership. There are, of course, the locked and loaded committed types, who go to the gym like many Christians attend church. It's what they believe in, therefore it's what they do, and no matter the weather, with the exception of holidays they'll be there working their bodies. But I've noticed there are two major spikes in new people joining the gym. The first is at the turn of New Year, usually coinciding no doubt with a New Year's resolution that includes losing weight! The second is in the build up to the summer holiday season; after all, if one is to wear a bikini or Speedos, one needs to have the body of a god! In most cases, it seems these bursts of enthusiasm don't last, and the spikes subside while the die-hards outlast them all. The issue for those who start and stop is not willpower, but vision. For them, exercise is a means to an end: "I want to loose weight", or "I want to look great!" Though there's nothing essentially wrong with such motivation, I guess it just isn't enough. This reduces exercise to an event, an add-on, and soon, an inconvenience. The danger is that once the magic weight is achieved or the belly flattens enough for the beach shorts, exercise is discarded; job done! Alternatively, if the weight doesn't drop off quickly enough or a barrel still occupies the place where the six-pack should be, they give up! It's truly not the lack of willpower that's the problem, but rather the smallness of the vision. If the driver becomes wellbeing instead of waistline, or healthiness instead of sex-appeal, then the vision will be bigger, the commitment longer and the result stronger. The goal will move from being about a number or a season, to a much better way of living.

As followers of Jesus we need to enlarge our vision when it comes to being strong. Waist size is not the primary issue, wellbeing is. The issue isn't how good we look, but rather how well we feel and how well we're doing. How ever we engage with physical exercise, the key factor is why we're doing what we're doing. In any sphere of life, in order to *become* we need a *because*. If our "because" is strong enough, then becoming is inevitable. It's not a case of if but when!

R-est and re-create

Jesus' disciples had just returned from their first ministry trip (without Him) and they were pumped. They wanted to share their excitement with Jesus and, no doubt, to get straight back out there and do more stuff. However, at that moment Jesus calls them to a radical change of gear:

Come with Me by yourselves to a quiet place and get some rest. (4)

In this simple statement Jesus demonstrates the power and necessity of rest and relaxation in the context of ministry if we are to serve consistently well. From this one statement we learn four key principles:

R&R is spiritual
"Come with Me..."
By going with His disciples, Jesus wasn't simply telling them what

to do, He was showing them how to do it. His actions endorsed His words and therefore gave legitimacy to the concept of rest. Jesus taught them that spiritual wisdom resides in physical rest.

R&R is relational

"... by yourselves..."

In this moment, Jesus demonstrated that it's possible to find rest and achieve the refilling of our heart's tank in the company of others. There are times when I need a little "cave time" to be on my own to rest and reflect, but there are other times when the opposite is required. I have discovered, for example, that good food with great friends is one of the most dynamic ways to rest, and by the end of such evenings my tank is often well and truly full! We'll come back to the relational growth of our lives later in this book, but suffice to say, the right friends in the right context will always produce uplift and strength.

R&R is emotional

"... to a quiet place..."

We live in a noisy world. It seems that everywhere we go noise fills the background and many times tries to dominate. How many times have you sat in a coffee shop and had to raise your voice because the music was so loud? As human beings we are living under greater levels of stimulus than ever before, and although we are remarkable in our ability to adapt and innovate, there are times when we need to turn down the dial, close the laptop, log out of Facebook and find a quiet place. As the crowd demanded more, Jesus sought a place of quietness in which His friends could recover and rejuvenate. Every now and again the world must wait as we learn to quieten our souls!

R&R is physical

"... and get some rest."

I feel no guilt over taking rest. I have trained my mind to think properly on this. All work and no play makes Jack... a ticking bomb! And when Irishmen explode, it's usually pretty spectacular! I have met a few people in my lifetime who have made rest an art form, and they need to learn to do a bit of work, but most of the people occupying the world in which I live and serve work very hard; sometimes too hard. It's okay to have a day off, even God had one! It's okay to take a moment in the coffee shop, have a walk in the park, watch a movie at the cinema, or spend a few extra hours in bed. It's not a sin. In fact, sometimes it's the most spiritual thing we can do. To burn for the Lord should be an ambition for all of us, but to *burn out* for Him is neither attractive to others nor glorifying to Him. With regular rest we can run further and longer.(5) Authentic rest will always lead to genuine re-creation!

Remember, finally...

R&R is optional

"Come..."

Jesus issued an invitation to His young disciples not a command, because He understood that rest cannot be forced, rather it must be embraced. Until rest becomes essential in our thinking, a concept rooted deep in the paradigm of our spirituality, then it will remain something we think about occasionally and do reluctantly. Left to their own devices, His disciples, excited by the fruit of their recent ministry trip, would probably have opted to press on and milk the moment for all it was worth. But Jesus knew better and offered them an alternative to the excitement and intoxication of the crowd. By inviting them to *come* He was giving them the power to *go*!

O-rder your time

As a boy in Sunday school I remember hearing the little maxim, "Those who fail to plan, plan to fail!"

There is a kernel of truth contained within this statement. Like so many issues in life, our physical development requires not only a vision, but a plan of action; a plan that is sustainable, practical and profitable. Exercise, rest, fun, and great connections won't and don't just happen, we have to make them happen. We must plan for them to happen and ensure that they do happen. As we've already seen, everyone arrives somewhere, but only some arrive on purpose!

When it comes to ordering, managing, or as I prefer to think of it, *leading* time, there are numerous packages and techniques out there to help us. However, in finding the best way to do it for me, and in seeking to help others over the years, I've identified some very simple principles as a guide. I think of them as four Ps:

Time leadership starts with Purpose, not time

Too often we try to manage time by getting our calendar out and trying to make everything fit. But before we open iCal or order that wall planner, we must address an even more fundamental question: *What is my purpose?* Now, I know that's a huge question, but it can be broken down.

What's my purpose within this job?
What purpose am I trying to achieve for my children?
What is my key purpose for this next year?
What is the purpose of my life?

Many people don't want to get to these questions, because they are difficult and sometimes painful. In every case, by addressing such questions we'll come to the realisation that we're trying to fit too much stuff into too small a purpose shape. However, there is no point paying any money for a time-management system until we've at least begun to answer the purpose question.

The purpose catalyses Priorities

Purpose will always naturally produce a series of priorities. They may be big-picture life priorities, or seasonal or contextual priorities, but whatever they are, they will start to highlight areas we need to say yes to, and others we need to say no to. Living in the power of *yes* empowers us to more easily say *no* to things that distract from our purpose. Learning to say no, truly releases us in the yes of our purpose. Too many say yes to everything and although they look busy and productive, tragically their activity can disguise the fact that they are saying no to the "everything" of purpose. Focused people are usually productive people and although we have to be careful not to become so blinkered that we shut our world out, still we must remember that "the more prepared we are, the more spontaneous we can be".

Priorities require Practicalities

There is no one way to time-lead, in fact I would encourage as much creativity and variety as possible depending on the context, the call and the character of the person. The worst thing we can do is simply copy someone else because they seem to be successful at this, without understanding the drivers and principles at the heart of their plan. Belief-drivers and principles will better equip us to design our own plan, so that the practicalities serve us, rather than boss us. The diary can be the master or the slave... you decide.

Don't forget your Personality

We're all different and we must not be afraid to acknowledge that our personality type has a bearing on how we do things. Again we can learn, adapt and change if need be, but a reasonable understanding of how we are wired and how we work best has got to be a good thing. The challenge is to lead-time in a way that reflects the best of our personality without compromising our purpose.

All of this is important when it comes to the physicality of our spirituality. If we don't see rest, relaxation, exercise, friendships, holidays and wellbeing as important – as part of our purpose – then none of these things will register as significant priorities in our lives and practically we just won't make time for them. If something is important to us, it's amazing what we'll be prepared to do to make it happen. If we conclude that our spirituality includes our physicality, then we'll order our time accordingly. There's always enough time for the things we ought to do!

N-utrition matters

I'm no expert on nutrition, but I know enough to understand that if we feed our bodies with junk it will start to negatively impact the finely tuned system that houses our spirit. On the other hand, if we feed our bodies with a well-balanced, blended diet that includes all the nutritional elements we require, we'll give our body every chance of staying healthy for longer. If we went to buy a car, very few would simply drive it and, on the basis of the drive alone, make the decision to buy. We'd ask questions, we'd want to know about fuel consumption, costs, service history and anything else relevant to ensure the car would run the best it could. We'd refer to the manufacturer's manual to help us understand how the car worked and get tips on how to make sure it stayed working.

So many people are oblivious to how their body works, what's good for it, what's bad, what makes it better and what can make it worse – yet it's the only body we've got! Usually we don't start taking diet and nutrition seriously until something goes wrong. But why wait until then?

I love food… eating is one of my favourite pastimes. I've long moved from food being a biological necessity to being a life-pleasure, and I'm blessed by a wife who is an amazing cook. But it is important to know what to eat and how much to eat because as we all know, what tastes good can actually be poisoning us! I'm not a healthcare professional, so I can't advise on the details of diet or the unique requirements of any one individual, but there are people out there who can help. Talk to your doctor, make an appointment with a nutritionist, and get some advice from one of those smart people who know how to make life work in this area and stop being naïve and stupid when it comes to food.

G-row good connections

Good, healthy connections with friends, people we love and people who love us, are crucial for our physical maturity. We tend to think of this in the context of emotional development, and I'll deal with that later in the book, but I believe it also has a powerful impact on our physical development. I read a fascinating book by Dr Caroline Leaf called *Who Switched off My Brain* and although I enjoyed the whole book and learned a heap of stuff, the price paid was worth it for just one chapter: Toxic Touch. Exploring the importance of healthy relationships and connections in our lives, she talks about "skin-hunger" and suggests:

"Touch is literally described as 'one of the most essential elements of human development,' a 'critical component of the health and growth of infants' and a 'powerful healing force.'" She found evidence that as far back as the 1940s, research demonstrated that babies were dying from 'touch-deprivation' and that those societies which display high levels of violence register as among the least physically affectionate on earth. Her evidence suggests that physical human connection with those who love us, releases the body's natural chemicals in a healing process that optimizes our feelings of wellbeing; that "affectionate touch" is an essential nutrient for our wellbeing. She concludes:

"...lack of touch (called 'cutaneous deprivation') causes emotional problems, affects our intellect and physical growth, and weakens our immune system. Research even shows touch-deprivation causes negative change in the brain (neuroplasticity), laying the patterns for aggression and violence."(6)

I have often said that, "the people around me make me look much better than I am" and it seems scientific research has shown that to be true. If we are to grow strong physically, grow deliberately in stature as Jesus did, then we must pay attention to the people we connect to and the results of their touch. A touch can bring bruises or blessing and we must seek to ensure that those we allow to touch our lives have only blessing in mind. It also challenges us to make a decision: only touch others to bless them!

Over the years I've come dangerously close to serious failure ignoring these sound principles for life and strength, and thought that I was clever enough to make it on my own. As Forest Gump said, "Mama says, stupid is what stupid does," and truly I've been both stupid and witnessed stupidity that ultimately weakens us and can potentially destroy us. Here are six ways to be stupid and reject S.T.R.O.N.G. living:

S-ay yes to everything
You can if you want to, but remember, busy doesn't mean better. Learn to work smarter, not harder!

T-hink burnout will never happen to you
Nobody who has experienced burnout ever thought it would happen to them, because deep down we all think we're invincible. Burnout is something that happens to others, but not me… well, think again and think now!

U-nderestimate the task
I love working for the Lord and I get to work for His Church and get paid for the privilege. But as much as I love it and believe it is my purpose to do it, I must not underestimate the power of this role to take over my life so that I end up exhausted, unhappy and useless. If we treat the task with a healthy respect, it will save us from arrogance and ignorance.

P-rioritise doing over being
It's so easy to be caught up in the value-system that is centred on what we do rather than who we are. Everywhere we go we're pressured to *do*, but learning to rest, stepping back from the day to day activity, giving time to our physical wellbeing, reminds us that there are some things more important than our "to do" list.

I-gnore the warning lights
When the light flashes on the dashboard it's for a reason. Don't ignore it, don't wait a week or convince yourself you'll get round to it, but rather ask the questions smart people ask: "Why is this flashing?" and "How can I fix it?"(7)

D-iscard good friends

Isolation is either a sign that something has gone wrong or a clear signal that something is about to go wrong. As we shall see, "no man is an island", so why behave like you are? Get over yourself and realise that the "affectionate touch" of friends will not only bring you life, but empower you to success.

God doesn't want us to be S.T.U.P.I.D. Rather, He wants us to be S.T.R.O.N.G. Jesus grew in stature, and today, we can make a decision to grow on purpose, so that ultimately we are "fit for purpose".

Study & Reflection

"And Jesus grew in stature..."
"For physical training is of some value, but godliness has value for all things..."

In what way has a misunderstanding of this verse impacted your life or church, directly or indirectly? Put another way, what's your attitude or that of your church to physicality when considered in the light of spirituality?

Spirituality includes physicality
"We need to intersect our work, home, community and sexuality with God... we must intermix the realms. Whatever God touches becomes sacred. Spirituality that isn't 24/7 is just hollow religion – a segregated component of a non-integrated person."

In what way might our attitudes and actions change towards our physicality if we saw it as part of our spirituality?

Train on purpose, for purpose
Why is it important to be motivated by wellbeing and not waist size; by how we feel rather than how we look?

Rest and Relax
Why is rest and re-creation so important for our wellbeing and spirituality?

What does rest and re-creation look like in your life and how could it improve?

Order your time
Do you see growth in stature as part of your purpose? If so, in what ways are you intentionally incorporating this into your lifestyle?

Nutrition matters
In the context of our spirituality and life-purpose, why is nutrition important?

Are there any areas around nutritional development with which you struggle? Identify them, seek expert advice and make the changes now.

Grow good connections
List the people you believe are "good connections" in your life. Now beside their name write the ways in which these people bring positive influence, especially in the area of physical growth and development. How does that look? Do you have people in your life who positively encourage your "stature-growth" as part of your purpose and spirituality?

Section 3:
Growing in God - SQ

6. Learning to be Spiritual

"And Jesus grew... in favour with God..."

It's hard to get our heads around the idea that Jesus grew in favour with God. How does God in flesh grow in favour with God? But as we've seen previously, Luke tries to demonstrate that Jesus the man (though never divorced from His God-ness), has to learn to grow so that He can fulfil the purpose God has called Him to. I love how NT Wright puts Luke 2:52 in his New Testament translation:

"So Jesus became wiser and taller, gaining favour both with God and with the people."(1)

It's easy to miss the word "became", but that's the "little" hinge on which this magnificent door turns. Without learning to *become*, Jesus would not have been ready for that which God had purposed – and within the 2:52 principle, this issue of growing in favour with God is perhaps the most paradoxical we have to address. But when it comes to biblical theology, paradox is our friend. When I first started to get to grips with the Bible, I wanted clear, concise answers to everything. I loved the idea of a book on systematic theology that allowed me to pick from my shelf an easy answer to hugely difficult ideas. At Bible College I was known for my more Calvinistic tendencies and could recite my TULIP doctrinaire off by heart. It was neat, it was clean, it was simple and I was in control! However, I've discovered that this is a very western modernist approach to understanding biblical truth, which represents a challenge when the Bible was written in a largely Eastern pre-modern world. I've come to discover that rather than the Bible running away from paradox, it clearly celebrates it, and I'm invited to wrestle with the tension of contradiction to find an answer. If ever the word paradox fitted a scripture it's this one. Luke leads us to a conclusion that seems "senseless, logically unacceptable and self-contradictory". Jesus grew in favour with God!

Before we consider how Jesus grew in favour, let's just take a moment to think about the idea of favour itself in this context. The word used here is *cháris*, which at a basic level points to the idea of graciousness, favour and gratitude.But within the New Testament it is often the context which determines its meaning. Thus a number of different nuances emerge from the word giving it glorious variety. For example, it can point to "attractiveness that invites a favourable reaction", "unmerited goodness", "a practical application of goodwill", "an exceptional effect produced by generosity", and "a response of gratitude to generosity".(2) However, Luke in his gospel has already used the word on two occasions previously and these verses help us to understand what might be going on in Luke 2:52.

The first reference is Luke 1:30:

But the angel said to her, "Do not be afraid Mary; you have found favour with God."

The second reference is Luke 2:40:

And the child grew and became strong; He was filled with wisdom, and the grace of God was on Him.

In the first reference to do with Mary the mother of Jesus, the favour, grace and generosity of God is clearly coming to her because of something she has done. Her attitudes and actions have attracted God's favour. Of course, we know she was a sexual virgin, but this could not be the only reason God took note of her – after all there must have been thousands of female virgins in her world at that time. Something else attracted God. We can see from Mary's "Magnificat" that this is a young woman with a strong faith, a clear knowledge of Scripture and a vibrant spirituality.(3) As Luke uses the word here in 1:30, he's clearly pointing to the reactive favour of God, coming to Mary in response to actions and attitudes that have attracted it.

In the second reference, the meaning is entirely different. Luke suggests that as Jesus grew, the grace of God was upon Him; not so much because of anything Jesus was doing, but rather as an action of God to Jesus, to help empower Him for the task ahead. In 2:40 the favour referred to here is more proactive than reactive. This has less to do with the attitude and actions of Jesus and everything to do with God's desire to bless, empower and encourage.

When it comes to the grace and favour of God we must again welcome paradox into our world. At one level, we have received God's "unmerited favour" not because of anything we have done, but because of everything He has done. We are children of God not through human will, or self-design, but because of the will of Him who loved and saved us. We are saved by His grace alone! This is God's "proactive favour" coming to us before we even realised we needed it and certainly without our deserving it.

But then there is another aspect to grace, seen in the life of Mary and contained, I believe within 2:52 – that of attractional grace or favour. This is something that God does for us and gives to us, as a result of our attitudes or actions. This is God's "reactive favour", bestowed on those who align themselves with Him, walking His way and doing as He commands. Jesus, like His mother, attracts the favour of God to His life and gets God's attention in such a way that God lavishes generous favour upon Him. What encourages me is that this word translated in this way isn't just used of Jesus, but of Mary too. If Luke only used it of

Jesus, we might conclude, "Ah well, that's Jesus", but we cannot make the same conclusion of Mary. She is just an ordinary young woman in her culture. She wasn't sinless, perfect or superhuman, yet she too attracted God's favour, just as Jesus the man did.

Jesus teaches us from this insight that our mindset and lifestyle can attract and, by implication, repel the favour of God. Of course, this understanding of this aspect of grace is fraught with dangers, stimulating the search for formulas and principles that press God's buttons and get Him to be extra especially good to us! This aspect of God's favour has been tragically abused by modern Christianity, creating a self-centred "bless-me" culture. Misunderstood, it gives Christians the excuse to be materially covetous and selfish on the grounds of spiritual obedience. We've reduced favour to postcodes, badges on cars and numbers in the bank, thus tempting ourselves to manipulate God by our lifestyle so that He will do what we want. Ironically, this mentality is the fast track to missing God's favour. If we make it our aim to please Him because we love Him, then His favour will hunt us down, all the days of our lives!(4)

The Father's favour to Jesus is explicitly expressed at His baptism. Luke tells us that as Jesus was being baptised, the Holy Spirit descended on Him in *"bodily form like a dove"* and a voice came from heaven, which said,

You are My Son, whom I love; with You I am well pleased.(5)

In this one statement, the Father expresses His favour to the Son in three dynamic ways.

Affirmation – "You are My Son..."

The identity of Jesus is affirmed to Him and all who might hear. There's a lovely little play on this from Luke in the genealogy of Jesus that immediately follows the record of this event.

*Now Jesus Himself was about thirty years old when He began His ministry. He was the son, **so it was thought**, of Joseph.(6)*

The Father confirms and affirms the identity of Jesus in a deeply personal way, "You are My Son…". Jesus' understanding of Himself is not seen in isolation, but in relationship to His Father. He is not only the Son of God, but He is the Son of the Father. I believe this is an affirmation, a public confirmation of what Jesus already knew. Jesus has already made reference to His "Father's house" and it seems that during the 18 years of silence, He grew in a clear understanding of not only who He was, but who His Father was and the power of that relationship.

Could it be that confidence in our God-given identity attracts God's favour to our lives? In a world that thinks John Andrews is the son of Alex and Ruth (though I celebrate this), I know I am a son of my Father in heaven and that my identity is not determined by my genetics or heritage, but by my heavenly Father! Does this delight the heart of the Father, when we get this, understand it and learn to truly live in it? I think it does. Imagine if every day one of my three children came to me and asked, "Am I yours?" Such a question, expressing such doubts, would ultimately serve to undermine love, trust and favour. When we question who we are we also question the One who made us and called us. Living under the tyranny of identity doubt repels God's favour from our lives. But when we simply trust and accept who we are and Who made us, even when surrounded by a cynical or sceptical world, we grant God permission to lavish us with His generous favour.

Acceptance – "…whom I love…"

This statement demonstrates that what the Father and Jesus have together is not merely functional, but relational; it is not a religious contract but an intimate covenant. The Father expresses love for

Jesus in tender and intimate terms, held up as His Beloved. If identity is at the core of the Father's affirmation, then intimacy saturates this loving acceptance of the Son.

I love how the Apostle John expresses the same idea for us: *See what love the Father has lavished on us, that we should be called children of God! And that is what we are!*(7)

John calls to us to stop and take a long hard look at the Father's love... Behold!

An understanding of how loved we are is crucial to living in the attractional favour of God. Too many believers are unsure if they are loved, how much they are loved and if God's love might change or run out on them. If the earth trembles at the reality of a "married woman who is not loved,"(8) how must the universe tremble when those who claim to carry His name and His Divine DNA are constantly wondering, "Does God really love me?" We can somehow accept the premise that God is love, that He doesn't just love as an action, that His love is the very expression of who He is, and yet still entertain thoughts that we're the exception, the unloved member of the family. How much must it please Him when we live loved? When we make a decision to accept His expression of love to us through Jesus and believe it no matter what. So often when something isn't working out, when life is tough, or we end up with the dirty end of the stick, we question His love and His commitment to us. Could it be that in the years of silence, where there were no miracles, signs, wonders or great opportunities, Jesus learned to live in the love of God, deliberately growing to access that love without strings or small print? As He helped at home, worked as a *tékton*, sat in the *bet midrash* and toiled under Roman oppression, I suggest to you He found His Father's love and made it the bedrock of His soul. Such confidence in His Father's love was attractive. If this is so, no wonder He grew in favour!

Approval – "...with You I am well pleased."

The word used here for well pleased is *eudokéō* and carries with it the idea of "thinking good of something"; considering something or someone as good and therefore worthy of choice and thus taking pleasure in it. Therefore, the pleasure the Father expresses for Jesus is deliberate and intentional. He has considered Jesus and given His life serious thought and His conclusions are that He thinks well or good of Him, and thus by implication, He is pleased with Him.

What an idea, that God would think well of us! This will make some nervous, the thought that anything we do could be considered good by God. I remember ministering somewhere and I said to a very helpful and generous gentleman, "You are a good man." His reply shot from his mouth like a bullet from a gun, "There is none good brother, only God." Again, paradox helps us here. How can a sinner be good in the eyes of God? How can one who has been saved by God's unmerited favour now attract favour because God has "thought well" of them? God thinks good of us as a choice of His will, motivated by His loving kindness, but Luke suggests that God also thinks good of us in response to what He sees in us, as we in turn have learned to respond to Him.

I love all of my children passionately and that is as much an act of my will as my emotion for them or my connection to them. I love them for who they are! However, recently in church, my oldest daughter was leading worship, my son was playing the drums and my youngest daughter was serving in the connections ministry. As I watched them do what they do with passion, faith and enthusiasm, I was pleased with them; I thought them good. If they weren't serving they'd still be loved and adored, but at that moment, their actions attracted me and caused me to think well of them.

At this point in history, as far as we know, Jesus hadn't healed anyone, preached any great sermons or announced Himself to the world, yet the Father was pleased with Him! I believe that the Father looked at the silent years, the 91% if you like, and was pleased by what He saw. He intentionally thought about Jesus and His thoughts were good!

This public expression of favour from the Father didn't just happen as a random and unrelated action. Rather it relates to the determination of Jesus to grow in the unseen and private places, settling His attitudes and plotting His course. John's gospel gives us an insight into Jesus' attitudes that may have caused the Father to express His favour in such a way. Although Jesus says the following words during His ministry, I believe it's not a stretch to suggest that the mentality they reflect was in Jesus before His public ministry began.

Take a look at John 5:19-20:

Very truly I tell you, the Son can do nothing by Himself; He can do only what He sees the Father doing, because whatever the Father does, the Son does. For the Father loves the Son and shows Him all He does. Yes, and He will show Him even greater works than these, so that you will be amazed.

Note the rooted-ness of Jesus' life in the Father and the reliance of His ministry upon the instruction and direction of the Father. Though separate, they are intertwined, and what is striking is that this is due to an attitude of submission from Jesus to the Father. I suggest to you, this didn't just start happening at Jesus' baptism, but this was happening in the silent years. Thus, having learned it in the 91%, it was natural in the 9%. But what does it teach us and how did it help Jesus to grow in favour?

Aligned to the Father – "...the Son can do nothing by Himself..."

Of course, this is strictly untrue, for had Jesus wanted He could have done a lot of things by and for Himself. However, Jesus made a choice – dare I say He learned a choice – and decided that His way needed to be aligned with the Father's purpose and so gave away His right to choose on any issue. The writer to the Hebrews is clear on this: *"Son though He was, He learned obedience from what He suffered"*, and that He was *"made complete and perfect..."*. (9) Undoubtedly part of that process in obedience would have been to learn to align His will to that of the Father.

How attractive is that? In an age where self is god and choice is everything, we are shocked and hopefully awed at the prospect of Jesus giving up His right to self-determination and the freedom of choice, in order to align Himself with someone else's agenda. This is what Jesus did as an example to us all. As He learned obedience, so can we. As He was made complete and perfect in the purposes of God, so can we be. But it all hinges on our attitude to who is king and whether our choices are His or ours.

If we truly learn to align, we will grow in favour with God.
Alignment attracts favour!

Agreement with the Father – "...He can do only what He sees the Father doing, because whatever the Father does the Son also does."

The Bible teaches us that *"two are better than one..."*(10), but of course that's only true when two agree as one! Agreement makes two better than one and agreement allows the power of two go further than even the sum of their abilities. Agreement is even built into the Godhead and without it God cannot operate.

Agreement has been designed into the very DNA of humanity, to such an extent that not only is it not good to be alone, but it is impossible to achieve the full limit of potential while standing alone. In Genesis 11 God makes an amazing statement about a group of people who were building a city and tower for selfish and potentially dangerous ends:

"If as one people speaking the same language they have begun to do this, then nothing they plan will be impossible for them."(11)

There is power in agreement!

Jesus learned this and grew in this. Jesus understood that He could not achieve everything He had been put on earth to do without agreeing with the Father. He could not do His own thing, He could not go His own course, and He could not be His own man. Jesus learned that though He could, He couldn't.

What wisdom, to agree with God for your life! God has been doing life a long time and yet a human being who has been on the planet five minutes, who struggles to fix a plug or understand a computer, has the audacity to try to make life work without input from the Creator and sustainer of the universe. That's not smart! The clever thing is to work out, "Where is God going?" and follow or to ask the question, "What does God want?" and do it! The more we agree with God the more we grow in favour. As we learn to agree we become attractive to the reactive favour of God and our lives become unimaginably enriched.

If we truly learn to agree, we will grow in favour with God. Agreement attracts favour!

Authority from the Father – "For the Father loves the Son and shows Him all He does..."

Jesus was able to speak with authority on behalf of the Father because He aligned and agreed with Him. A Gentile soldier understood this and in the process, I believe, had a revelation of who Jesus truly was. In Luke 7 we have the story of a Roman centurion who not only loved the Jewish nation, building a synagogue in his vicinity, but he valued his servant, a highly unusual thing in the 1st century world. The servant was sick and the request sent for Jesus to come and heal him. As Jesus was on the way, the centurion sent word and said,

Lord, don't trouble Yourself, for I do not deserve to have You come under my roof... but say the word and my servant will be healed. For I myself am a man under authority, with soldiers under me. I tell this one, "Go," and he goes; and that one "Come," and he comes. I say to my servant "Do this," and he does it.

This Roman understood how authority worked. In order to have it, you must be under it! As he looked at Jesus he recognised two things: namely, the authority that Jesus had, and where it came from. In recognising both these things, is it possible that this Gentile saw Jesus' Messianic authority? Look at how Jesus responds:

I tell you, I have not found such great faith even in Israel.(12)

Jesus was not simply impressed by the Roman's faith, after all, many had faith in Israel at the time and many up to this point had already been healed, but not everyone recognised where the authority to heal came from. However, this man did and it's that which Jesus is commending... not just his faith, but his vision.

Jesus had authority because He was under authority. He learned to be under the authority of His Father in the silent years so when He takes the stage of His ministry, He operates with comfort and ease. He is able to act with authority because He is under authority.

In the same way the centurion impressed Jesus and attracted His favour, seen in the healing of his servant. So Jesus impressed the Father by grasping one of the greatest life and leadership principles of all: to have authority one must submit to authority. Jesus could only give as He received, could only lead because He followed, and could only speak because He listened. This attitude attracted the Father's gaze and favour and, in the same way, such an attitude distilled in our lives can have the same effect.

**If we truly learn to live under authority,
we will grow in favour with God.
Authority attracts favour!**

It's easy to look at Luke 3:22 and hear the words of the Father, affirming, accepting and approving the Son, and find ourselves caught up in the moment while missing entirely the process. When we connect the Father's expression of favour to Jesus at His baptism, to the words of Jesus in John 5:19, words that can't just apply to His ministry, but must refer to His pre-ministry life, we are truly not surprised. For in the silent years and throughout His ministry years, Jesus learned to align Himself to the Father, walk in agreement with the Father and operate in authority from the Father. I submit to you that as Jesus deliberately and intentionally grew in alignment, agreement and authority, it was inevitable that He would attract the favour of the Father.

Jesus learned to grow in favour... and so can we!

Study & Reflection

"And Jesus grew in favour with God..."

Growing in favour with God seems to present a paradox to us. What is a paradox and how can it help us get to grips with biblical truth? Can you think of any other Bible paradoxes?

In this chapter we talked about God's "proactive grace" and His "reactive favour". From Luke 1:30, apart from her sexual virginity, what factors in Mary's life might have attracted God's "reactive favour" to Mary?

From Luke 2:40, how might God's "proactive grace" have assisted Jesus as He grew in His childhood?

From Luke 3:22 and the words of the Father to Jesus at His baptism, we considered the following:
- Affirmation – identity
- Acceptance – intimacy
- Approval – intention

Why would these issues be attractive to the Father?

What is it about them He might like and respond to?

Read John 5:19-20

Jesus aligned Himself to the Father. Look again at Hebrews 5:8-9. How might Jesus have learned obedience and in what way was He made perfect or complete?

Jesus agreed with the Father. We were encouraged to ask two questions:
Where is God going?
What does God want?
At a practical level, how can we learn to discern the answer to these questions?

Jesus lived with authority from the Father. Look again at Luke 7:1-10 and consider this statement: "In order to have authority, we must be under authority."

What does this teach us about authority?

Can you think of any modern life examples of this principle?

Why is authority an important issue in our followership of Jesus?

7. Inside Out

"And Jesus grew... in favour with God..."

I was at the gym recently pumping away on the cross-treader when I noticed an advert for a fitness programme on one of the numerous TV screens. Though I couldn't hear the words, I caught the gist. It looked like a civilian version of an army boot camp and all those participating were clearly trying their hardest to look happy. Lots of trim, sweaty, beautifully sculpted bodies were jumping, pumping and stomping with the promise that I could have a body just like theirs, if only I had this programme, for a ridiculous amount of cash, with a sixty-day money back guarantee. However, what really caught my attention was the various tag lines flashing up, such as, "beach body", "body beautiful" and "the body you've always wanted". The emphasis was on *looks* not *life*, appealing to my vanity and offering the promise that I too could have a rippling six-pack. The pitch was shamelessly aimed at the superficial because that's what people see. That's the part a shallow, self-absorbed culture judges us on, so that's the bit we have to fix. Whatever else is going on in my life, as long as I look good, that's all that matters!

Our spirituality can fall into the same trap. As human beings we're obsessed with the outward, whereas God is primarily interested in the inward. It is not that the outward aspect of our lives is unimportant to God, far from it, but He is looking for outward actions that are an authentic expression of what lives on the inside. The danger with any religious journey is that we can learn what to do and when to do it. We know what it takes to look good in certain contexts and we can seamlessly slip into a double life – one where the inner life has no bearing whatsoever on the outer life. An unholy and dangerous disconnection can begin to develop in our lives where we handle the bankruptcy of our inner experience with clever management of our behaviour. We're all tempted to do it, but the more we do it and get used to doing it, the easier it becomes to live a double life where our spirituality is divided up into religious and secular; where our lives divide into private and public and where our behaviour becomes authentically hypocritical; pretending to be someone on the outside that does not exist on the inside.

Listen to the guidance the Bible gives us on this:

*"Above all else, **guard your heart**, for it is the wellspring of life."*(1)

Solomon prioritises one thing over everything else: *the heart.* He urges us to guard it because it forms the source of our lives and shapes the boundaries in which we live. In other words, the quality of our inner life, our devotion to God, or as Luke puts it, growing in "favour with God", determines how well we live and how expansive or restrictive our lives are. Solomon teaches us that it's not what is around us that sets the spiritual temperature for our lives, but what's inside us. It's not our environment that shapes the boundaries of our lives, but our **in**vironment! Solomon is teaching us the importance of the *inside out* principle.

*Do not conform any longer to the pattern of this world, but **be transformed by the renewing of your mind**. Then you will be able to test and approve what God's will is — his good, pleasing and perfect will.*(2)

Paul is more or less saying, in a New Testament context, what Solomon said hundreds of years before. The key to living a life that is strong enough to resist being conformed to the philosophical pattern of the planet, is to have our minds renewed; to literally allow God's truth to "rewire" our heads, so we learn to think differently, thus empowering us to be *transformed*: changed in our behaviour and lifestyle. Paul reminds us that no matter how strong and persuasive the world around us is, the key to beating it is through a dynamic inner life with a *mindstyle* that impacts lifestyle. Paul is teaching us the importance of the *inside out* principle.

*Dear friend, I pray that you may enjoy good health and that all may go well with you, **even as your soul is getting along well**.*(3)

I like how the New King James puts it:

*Beloved, I pray that you may prosper in all things and be in health, **just as your soul prospers**.*

I love the picture behind the word translated *prosper*. The word is *euodóō* and is made up of two words, *eu* – good or well, and *hodos* – a road or by implication progress. Put the two together and we get the lovely idea that prosperity means to have the help we need for the journey; we have help on the road. Again, note the emphasis here from John. Though he wants them to be well in health and life, the benchmark he sets is that of the prosperity of the soul. In so doing, I believe he gives us two subtle hints. Firstly, we must not neglect the inner in preference for the outer. The health and wellbeing of the soul, our inner life, is crucial to the success of our journey. But secondly, if the wellbeing of our outer world and our physical health directly reflected the prosperity and health of our inner being, what would that look like? If our physical and material prosperity correlated to our spiritual vibrancy, would that be a cause for celebration or despondency? Like Solomon and Paul, John is teaching us the importance of the *inside out* principle.

Though this is not specifically aimed at leaders, it is a call to self leadership, so for the remainder of this chapter I'll be drawing on some insights, aimed at leaders, but relevant to anyone wishing to lead their own heart well, who wants to learn to live in God's attractional favour. John Maxwell suggested that, "If you can become the leader you *ought* to be on the *inside*, you will be able to become the leader you *want* to be on the *outside*."(4) Miller concurs when he concludes, "God always works on us from the inside out. He first changes us inwardly; then the outward actions begin to change."(5) Just as we saw in the previous chapter, the primary emphasis was on the development of the inner life, allowing Jesus to contend with the rigours of the call that His Father had placed on Him. Had the inner life of Jesus been lacking, the extreme demands of His public ministry would have surely found it out.

In the village where I ministered in my first church, plans were approved for some new houses and they just happened to be close to the pathway between our home and the local school our children attended. As I walked by on numerous occasions, there always seemed to be lots of people at work, but it was hard to see the evidence of their labour. For weeks, most of the work seemed to be below ground and out of sight. Massive energy and expense was expended to dig and lay the right foundations for the new houses. However, it seemed to take forever. Then we went away for a few weeks and when we returned, the walls of the houses were half built in a fraction of the time it took to lay the foundations. Yet, the only bit people really cared about was what the house looked like, how many rooms it had, the size of the kitchen and whether there was enough room for a 50inch TV. No one truly concerns themselves with the foundations, until of course something goes wrong. Yet, without well-designed, well-built, strong foundations, everything we see and enjoy would not be possible and would soon crack and crumble.

So many today are in a rush to build the house. They want everyone to "see" how well they are doing, how great they are and how much they've achieved. But as we're building the walls, adding new rooms and raising the levels, we need to soberly remind ourselves that if serious work hasn't be done in the foundations of our lives, sooner or later, cracks will appear in our lovely house and the pressure of life and ministry may cause it to crumble and fall. Miller reminds us: "Before we can conquer the world, we must first conquer the self... Many who drop out of ministry are sufficiently gifted, but have large areas of life floating free from the Holy Spirit's control. Lazy and disorganized people never rise to true leadership."(6) Jesus calls us to dig down deep and lay a good foundation.(7)

In his best selling book *The 7 Habits of Highly Effective People*, Covey alludes to the dynamic of the inside-out paradigm,(8) lamenting the fact that much of modern leadership has moved from a character ethic that is *substance driven*, to a personality ethic that is much more *style driven*, ruled by the sound-bite and romanced by the camera. The logic states that if leaders/people look good, followers initially care less about their policies and programs.(9) I saw this powerfully illustrated in the 1960 Nixon verses Kennedy US Presidential debate, the first of its kind held to be televised. (I wasn't born until 1966, but I've since watched the footage). For the first debate Nixon made a number of crucial mistakes, little things that added up to a big thing. For example, he campaigned up to a few hours before the debate started. He had just come out of hospital and therefore looked pale and underweight. He refused to wear make-up for the cameras and therefore his stubble was clear for all to see on the black and white screen. In fact, he looked so bad that on finishing the debate his mother rang him and asked if he was sick! By contrast, Kennedy had rested. He was fit, relaxed, handsome and tanned (even in black and white) beside the pasty looking Nixon. An estimated

70 million people watched the debate that night and their overwhelming conclusion was that Kennedy won hands down. Interestingly, a poll conducted among those who listened to the debate on radio said Nixon won. Nixon learned from his mistake and for the next three televised debates he put on weight, wore make up and tried to match Kennedy's style. But with on average 20 million less viewers tuning in... the damage was done.

The danger in life and leadership is that we succumb to the seductive allure of style – a relatively easy route to take. However, as we've seen in the life of Jesus (and the call comes to us as His followers), we must not substitute style for substance or allow our outer world to take priority over our inner life. After all, "There is no real excellence in all this world which can be separated from right living."(10) God's attractional favour comes to those who ensure the outside is an authentic expression of the inside!

Inside out – the choice is yours

"Have nothing to do with godless myths and old wives' tales; rather, **train yourself to be godly."**(11)

Paul writing to his son in the faith and a leader within the church at Ephesus, urges Timothy to "train" himself. The word used here is *gumnázō* and was commonly used of gymnastic exercises, often conducted naked. By implication it carries with it the thought of disciplined and focused training with literally no distractions or hindrances. Paul wanted Timothy to take his self-training seriously. As Maxwell says, "The first person you lead is you."(12) If we cannot lead ourselves in a vibrant spirituality, we'll struggle to authentically lead others. It's the difference between a tour guide and a travel agent. A travel agent knows the destination and knows how to get us there, but might not actually have been themselves. Thus they end up selling a brochure rather than an experience. A tour guide, however, doesn't simply send us; rather, he or she takes us. They know where they are going, they know how to get there and they know what it looks like, because they have been that way before. Thus, they are able to lead with authenticity and confidence.

When it comes to leading others we must remind ourselves to be spiritual first, leaders second. As Nelson puts it, "Human nature and the demeanour of leading mean that if leadership is the first priority, spirituality will be a very distant second. Such leading will lack spiritual potency."(13) All of us face the danger of pouring our energy into others, or even into the superficial, while at the same time neglecting personal foundations and inner development. It is not an either/or but rather a both/and situation. We have the responsibility to ensure that we train ourselves, keep the fire of God burning in our hearts, and that our lifestyle is an authentic expression of our soulstyle. Who we are is our responsibility! We cannot abdicate this to anyone else.

"Leaders choose to grow or not to grow. Both decisions are ultimately deliberate. Choices can place the leader's heart in God's hands for shaping as he sees fit."(14)

Inside out – the challenge is relentless

Bill Hybels concluded that *you* are your toughest leadership challenge.(15) It would be lovely to think that we could attend one intensive at a college or training school and get this module out of the way. In July 2017 I passed a huge ministry landmark of being in full-time paid Christian ministry for 30 years. Yet today, I have to be as intentional with my inner life as I did back at the beginning. I still have to make time for God's Word and ensure I'm cultivating a sensitive heart that keeps my Celtic cynicism at bay. I still have to apply discipline to "guard my heart" and "train myself". I'm still attending God's gym regularly and still there are times when I let myself down in attitude, thoughts and actions. Issues I thought I'd killed rise again to torment me; challenges within my masculinity and humanity taunt me; and at the heart of it all, my selfish ego lurks for an opportunity to spring a coup and take the throne of my heart. One would think that after 30 years that class is out, but I've discovered that although my life reflects a consistency and strength that arises out of godly principles, I still have to pay attention to the details, keep building the walls of protection, and refuse to believe my own PR. For me, the class is out, but it's also still on! Nelson, speaking to leaders, but applicable to all, puts it powerfully when he concludes, "... the most effective leaders invest significant time and energy making sure the 'axe is sharp' – that they are well read and that their mind, body, and soul are at their best. When the inner leader becomes depleted, it adversely affects everything the leader touches. When the inner leader is nourished, the entire organization benefits."(16)

If this is so, then we must intentionally devote time, resources and creativity to ensure that the axe of the inner self is sharp and that our hearts are still passionate for His presence, His word and His purpose. As Spurgeon said, "The most needful and profitable labour is that which we spend upon our own mental and spiritual improvement."(17) He added, "Spiritual fuel typically has a short shelf life. Our spiritual batteries only keep charge for so long. We need to recharge them whether they're used or not."(18)

I'd love to say that developing an inside-out lifestyle is a one-off hit, an easy, off-the-shelf programme, but it isn't. Jesus demonstrated in His own life that 91% was spent growing and strengthening the key areas of His life which attracted the Father's attention. This didn't stop when He started His ministry. Even Jesus had to continuously train Himself.

Inside out – the competency for the journey

"Watch your life and doctrine closely. Persevere in them, because if you do, you will save both yourself and your hearers."(19)

The word translated "watch" has a lovely nuance attached to it. The word is *epéchō* and carries the thought of holding and maintaining a tight grasp of something. In this context Timothy is encouraged to be "mindful and especially observant" of his own life. This is not to be a casual exercise of a passing glance, rather Paul wants concentrated effort and a firm grasp of what is going on. Many demands will be put on the young leader from many different quarters, and because of this Paul reminds him not to take his eye off his inner life and his growth in God.

But how do we do this?

When Moses was preparing God's people to enter the Land of Promise, he introduced them to what has become known as the Shema:

Hear, O Israel: The Lord our God, the Lord is One. And you shall love the Lord your God with all your heart and with all your soul and with all your strength. (Deuteronomy 6:4-5)

At the heart of these magnificent words are a revelation of who God is and an appropriate response to that revelation. As long as Israel kept Him at the centre, they would be strong. In essence, the Shema was a national call to inside-out living and remains a powerful guide to us in the 21st Century. In response to His greatness, there are five elements that are worthy of note as we seek to live inside out:

From Command to Response

*"**And** you shall love..."*

The inclusion or exclusion of just one word in the way this phrase is translated can make a huge difference to how we *hear* what the Lord is asking for. When the word "and" is excluded, the Shema becomes a command from God. But when "and" is included, the Shema becomes a response to God. The phrase is *ve'ahavta* and literally reads, "*and* you shall love", which seems to make greater sense in the light of what has gone before. Having heard that the "Lord our God the Lord is One", surely what comes next must be a response to that truth... "and". Love cannot be demanded nor commanded, but rather it must come from a heart free to hear and choose. Worship cannot be forced or coerced and should come from a heart that expresses in words and actions the revelation it has truly heard.

Inside-out living cannot be manipulated or manufactured, but is created out of what we hear and see for ourselves. We cannot worship from another's wonder and we must not succumb to the pressure of peers nor the folly of fake. The Shema is not a command, but a response, for the Lord desires that our love comes from faith not fear, from authenticity not pretence, and from revelation not information. That's why "and" is vital, because it connects revelation to response!

From feeling to knowing

*"And **you shall love**..."*

The phrase "And you shall love..." in English comes from one word in the Hebrew Bible, namely *ve'ahavta*, and it contains the verb to love, *'āhaḇ*. Though feelings are not excluded from the many nuances within the word, this love runs deeper than our feelings and goes beyond our emotions. In fact, to love in this way doesn't require feelings and emotion, they are a bonus feature to the main heartbeat of the word. To love is to act lovingly towards someone or something and to be focused, faithful and loyal. Love is not about what I feel, but about what I do. Love is less about emotion and more about action. Whatever or whoever I love will be evidenced in the way I behave towards that thing or person.

Words are easy to learn and rehearse, but actions are harder to fake in the long run. How we act towards the Lord is the true indicator of our love for Him. Though the Shema contains some of the greatest words ever penned, it is more than words to be learned and more than poetic literature to be enjoyed, for the Shema is a call to loving obedience as demonstrated in our actions. According to the Shema, when it comes to inside-out living, actions speak louder than words.

From fringe to centre

"... with **all your heart**..."

When it comes to the heart we must be careful not to be distracted by biological geography, but rather see this as a call to attitudinal alignment, for at stake here is the posture of the engine room of our inner world toward the Lord. The word "heart" *lēbāb*, can of course point to our physical heart, but over and over again within the Hebrew Bible it draws us to the core of a person's being, the inner workings of the mind and the centrality of the individual. As alluded to earlier in this chapter, Solomon teaches us that our **in**vironment determines our environment, laying claim to a paradigm that the condition of our inner world is of more importance and consequence than the realities around us.

The heart speaks of centrality and in this context we are being called to place Him at the centre of everything, thus allowing Him to be the Lord of every facet of our lives. To love the Lord with "all our hearts" is to position Him at the centre of our sexuality, family, finance, career and ambitions, and thus to refuse to allow any area of our experience autonomy from His authority. Centrality means that whatever He wants He can have and whatever He needs we will give.

We live in a world where so many ask the questions, "Who am I and why am I here?" These may be deemed useful questions to ask, but dangerously, *I* is at the centre of this enquiry, with life becoming a quest towards self-satisfaction. The Shema, however, calls us to ask two deeper and much more significant questions, namely: "Who is the Lord and what does He want?" He is at the centre, therefore our lives must be interpreted in the light of His position, person and purpose. This tendency to place self at the centre can creep into our worship, our service and our ambitions. Without even realising it, our behaviour starts to reflect Meology rather than Theology, where a dangerous shift sees the Lord serving us when we should be serving Him. When I is at the centre, God starts to look like us, shaped in our image. But when He is at the centre, we start to look like Him, moulded into His image.

From Casual to Intentional

"... with all your soul..."

The word translated soul is *nepeš*, and the first time we see it used is in Genesis 2:7 where we read:

Then the Lord God formed a man from the dust of the ground and breathed into his nostrils the breath of life, and the man became a living being.

The NIV translates it here as *being* and some translations use *soul*. The implication is that as God's "breath of life" entered the physical form of the man, he became a living being. In other words, according to the Genesis account, humans owe their *being* to *God's breath*. In the light of the revelation of who the Lord is, we are called to love Him with "all our souls" by giving back to Him the life that He gave to us. To love Him in this way is to surrender ourselves to Him, so that the life we have returns to the original purpose for which it was made.

Paul picks up this very idea when writing to the believers in Rome:

Therefore, I urge you, brothers and sisters, in view of God's mercy, to offer your bodies as a living sacrifice, holy and pleasing to God— this is your true and proper worship. (Romans 12:1)

Note the progression: "In view of... offer... worship."

True inside-out living starts with surrender. We do not surrender because we have to, but because we want to, and our surrender is not because we fear God, but because we love Him. Voluntary, willing, generous surrender to the Lord is beautiful to Him, having voluntarily, willingly and generously given us our life in the first place.

From Good to Best

*"... with **all your strength**."*

The word translated "strength" is *me'ōḏ* and can literally mean *very* or *muchness* and points to force, energy, strength, might and enthusiasm. To summarise, perhaps we're being asked to love God with the very best of who we are and what we've got. This idea is represented beautifully in the Creation account, when we're told: *"God saw all that he had made, and it was **very** good..."* (Genesis 1:31)

God's "good" in this context was *me'ōḏ*, the best of Himself given to creation in general and humanity specifically. In the light of the revelation of who the Lord is, we are called to love Him with "all our strength" by giving Him the best of ourselves in the very best way we can. Having given His best to us in creation and in salvation He deserves our *strength*. So many give what is left over, the dregs of what our day, creativity and energy has to offer, but the Shema calls us to give the best of all we are. Giving Him our best is the authentic expression of inside-out living.

Jesus lived inside out and as a result attracted the favour of God in His life. He deliberately grew in the principles that would help Him walk as a friend of God. So it is with us. We must learn to live inside out, understanding the importance and power of the inner life and the biblical truth that **in**vironment will trump environment every time. If we learn to guard our hearts by keeping Him at the centre, then our lives will grace our world and the prosperity of our souls will give us all we need for the journey before us.

If Jesus grew in favour with God... so can you!

Study and Reflection

"And Jesus grew in favour with God..."

In what ways can we allow our spirituality to become fixated on superficial issues?

How easy is it to pretend on the outside that everything is okay on the inside?

Look at the following verses:

Proverbs 4:23
In what ways can our heart be both the source and boundary of our lives?

Romans 12:1-2
How can we allow the Word of God to renew our minds? Can you think of an example in which this has already happened to you?

3 John 2

If your material and physical prosperity directly correlated to the level of your soul prosperity, would your life be richer or poorer, better or worse?

The Choice is Yours

"The first person you lead is you."

When it comes to your spiritual growth, are you leading or just letting it happen?

The Challenge is relentless

"Our spiritual batteries only keep charge for so long."

What tends to drain your batteries and in what ways are they recharged? How would you describe your battery life right now and why?

The Competencies for the journey

Give God first place. Look at again at the 3 Ps under this heading and consider: is God truly first in your life? I know you believe He is, but from your passion, purpose and priorities, can it be proven?

Think about our responses as recorded in the Shema.

How can I practically place the Lord at the centre of everything?

What does giving Him our best look like when translated into the practicality of our money, jobs, family and ministry?

Section 4:
Growing in Community - EQ

8. A People Person

"And Jesus grew... in favour with man."

One of the things I love to do as part of my devotionality is to continuously rotate the gospels, thus ensuring ongoing engagement with the life, ministry and teachings of Jesus. This has served as a rich source of inspiration and through it I have found my love for and worship of Jesus deepen and intensify. I have come to love the "red bits" of the Bible!(1) However, reading through the accounts of Jesus I am also struck by the connectedness of Jesus to people. Though it's too much of a stretch to say that Jesus was always surrounded by people, one gets the impression that Jesus was profoundly comfortable with them. Jesus, it seems, was a people person. However, the temptation is that we assume He was so because He was God in flesh, and one would assume that God is good with people. To accept this conclusion is to zero out the fact that Jesus spent His pre-ministry life living with people, getting to know them and, dare I say it, learning to love them. Luke makes it clear that Jesus deliberately and intentionally grew in such a way that His life attracted the favour of people around Him. I know we tend to target those who opposed Jesus, but when we consider the extensive and influential nature of His ministry, in truth He attracted far more favour than opposition. By and large, people seemed to like Jesus.

Consider the insights we get of Jesus as a "people person" from even a casual glance at the gospels.

Firstly, the assortment of people He connected with

The range of people in Jesus' world is breathtaking and He never seems on the back-foot in any context, bringing a level of personal security and comfort to each encounter.

Racial connection

Jesus made it clear that His primary focus in ministry was to save the "lost sheep of Israel".(2) Within that it's not surprising that most of His connections are with those from a Jewish background. But on many occasions He steps beyond that racial boundary to impact those not like Him. Jesus engages with Romans,(3) Samaritans,(4) Greeks(5) and a Syro-Phoenician(6).

Gender connection

In the context of the male dominated culture of His day, we see numerous examples of Jesus connecting to men, but what is fascinating is His comfort with women. Luke's gospel highlights this with the interplay between male and female in the ministry of Jesus. For example, in chapter 4 He heals a demoniac and Peter's mother-in-law. In chapter 7 He helps the centurion and the widow. In chapter 13 He talks of the man with the mustard seed and the woman with the leaven and at the end of the same chapter, and into chapter 14 He heals the woman bent double and the man with dropsy. Then in chapter 15 in speaking of lost things, He uses the example of a man who lost a sheep and a woman who lost a coin. In the same gospel women were identified as part of Jesus' disciples,(7) Jesus often used them as heroes within His stories,(8) He's seen teaching them and allowing them to learn,(9) He proclaims a woman to be a "daughter of Abraham" (the only time this happens in the whole of the Bible)(10) and women were clearly present when Jesus spoke of His death and resurrection and were a key part of the inner circle at the resurrection.(11) In fact, throughout the gospels we have approximately 112 passages relating to women!

Material connection

The impression created around Jesus is that He didn't like rich people, but the gospels show us this is simply not true. Many of the meals we see Him eating at would have been hosted by people who had the means to entertain and Jesus is as comfortable with them as He is with the poor. Undoubtedly He challenged attitudes to wealth and poverty, but there is not a single example of Jesus rejecting someone on the basis of their material condition. He is neither intimidated by wealth nor attracted to poverty. He learned to engage with both and did so with authenticity!

Religious connection

Again the impression is that Jesus didn't really like the religious, but Luke's gospel demonstrates something different. Luke's record, is amongst other things, famous for the amount of meals Jesus attends. I like how Karris puts it: "In Luke's gospel Jesus is either going to a meal, at a meal, or coming from a meal. In Luke's gospel Jesus got himself killed because of the way he ate."(12) Slight exaggeration perhaps, but point taken! The perception is that Jesus only ate with sinners,(13) but there are also at least 3 examples of Jesus eating with the religious.(14) When teaching my students from Luke's gospel, I suggest to them that Jesus was a "charismatic Pharisee" and that the religious were hanging around Him so much because they wanted to save Him, not because they hated Him. Most of them recognized that He was a "man sent from God", but they just couldn't get Him. We must not confuse Jesus' disagreement with the religious establishment as hatred of them. In fact, the evidence suggests He engaged with them almost as much as He did with sinners!

Margins connection

In the days of Jesus, many people lived on the margins of society and religion. Not only were they "bottom of the food chain" but they felt the pressure of a religion that seemed to suggest that God blesses the good and His blessing is a sign of goodness. So for those not experiencing God's goodness, they found themselves moved to margins. Within Israel the sort of people sitting in this group were:

Peasants – mainly rural dwellers. They suffered under various levels of hard labour. They were known to be the ones producing the majority of the food used in the area and yet they did not reflect that economically. This group included shepherds, farmers, tenants and day labourers.

The Unclean and degraded – including the sick, the demonized, prostitutes and those from other ethnic backgrounds.

The Expendables – those of no value to society including widows.

Women – especially those from the peasant, unclean, degraded and expendable backgrounds.(15) Look through this list and you'll notice one thing they all had in common: Jesus connected to all of them! As Karris concludes, "...Jesus should not be making friends with those who are not His own kind, that is, with toll collectors and sinners. Jesus' conduct is scandalous."(16)

The temptation is that we see Jesus' behaviour through a purely missional lens. Without denying this truth, I'd like to challenge the narrowness of this interpretation. The staggering range of people Jesus touched not only demonstrates the power of His mission but how good He was with people. He wasn't driven by a quota but by genuine love and concern for them.

Secondly, the ability He demonstrated when connecting

Observe the skills Jesus employs when ministering and connecting to people. Let's take one example from each area of His range, which we've previously looked at to highlight the depth of His ability.

Racial

Open up your Bible and read Matthew 8:5-13.

As you read the story, take notice of the simple "human" things Jesus does.

- He received him – remember the racial and political context! (vs. 5-6)
- He responded to him – *"Shall I come and heal him?"* (v7)
- He saw the good in him (v10)
- He helped him (v13)

Gender

Open up your Bible and read John 4:1-26.

As you read the story, take notice of the simple "human" things Jesus does.

- He asked for help (v7)
- He deflected away what divided (vs. 9-10)
- He respected and listened to her opinion and position (vs. 19-20)
- He didn't judge her (vs. 17-18)

Material

Open up your Bible and read Luke 19:1-10

As you read the story, take notice of the simple "human" things Jesus does.

- He came to where Zacchaeus was (v5)
- He knew/remembered his name (v5)
- He found a way of inviting Himself into his world (v5)
- He went into his house (vs. 6-7)
- He didn't judge him (vs. 9-10)

Religious

Open up your Bible and read John 3:1-15
As you read the story, take notice of the simple "human" things Jesus does.

- He received him with respect (vs. 1-2)
- He answered his questions (vs. 5-8)
- He challenged his thinking (v 9)
- He gave him space to work it out – He doesn't force Nicodemus to a conclusion.

Margins

Open up your Bible and read Luke 7:11-17
As you read the story, take notice of the simple "human" things Jesus does.

- He noticed her (v13) "When the Lord saw her…"
- He felt for her (v13) "… His heart went out to her…"
- He comforted her (v13) "Don't cry."
- He helped her (v15) "… and Jesus gave him back to his mother."

In all of the examples above, it is so easy to rush to the missional and miraculous punch line of the story and I am not in any way attempting to distract from that. However, as I've tried to illustrate (and I could have used dozens more examples), we must not miss the wonderful "human moments" in these stories. Jesus doesn't approach people generically with a "one-size fits-all mentality";

rather He connects with them where they are and in their context. Each approach and conversation is totally different, because each person is different. Jesus learned and employed a range of skills to allow Him (and His message) to get close to people. He won people over because He knew what people were like. I challenge you as you next read any of the stories of Jesus: spot His human skills not just His supernatural gifts. As you do so you'll discover He really was a people person!

Luke tells us in 2:52 that Jesus grew in favour with God and with men. We've already considered how the attitude and actions of Jesus' life attracted God's favour, so could it be the same principle applies when it comes to people? Jesus lived in such a way that somehow made Him attractive to people without compromising on belief and purpose. During the 91% He didn't just live with people, but He learned about them, so that during the 9% He could effectively connect and communicate with them.

What then made Jesus accessible to people and what attracted their favour?

It's difficult, of course, to answer this question explicitly from the silent years of His life, but if His ministry years are anything to go by, then we are able to identify some very strong clues of the type of behaviour that induced favour.

He liked people

We know and believe that Jesus in obedience to the Father came to save the world and that the motivation for that plan was God's love for us,(17) but because of that, it's easy to think that Jesus acted in a pre-programmed way, where His emotions and feelings were already set by the divine impulse of love. Though I believe in His *Godness*, He never stopped loving the world. I also believe as a man He had to learn to love those around Him and deal with the good, bad and ugly aspects of humanity. Great teachers love their students and great leaders love their followers. This greatness is not just about intelligence, innovation and information, but about a genuine desire to see others grow and prosper.

A few years ago an inspector sat in one of my classes in Bible College. After the class he asked if he could walk with me while we chatted. We exchanged a few pleasantries and then he said something which got my attention very quickly. He said, "You clearly love your students." I smiled and agreed, but then I asked him how he knew that. He answered, "By the way you talk to them, engage with them, listen to them and respect them. They enjoy learning in your class because you love teaching them." He then told me of his experience in seminary. He said that one of his theology teachers would enter the class, walk to the lectern, open his notes and begin to read them. In all that time he said, the lecturer would not look at the students or engage with them in any meaningful way. Then at the end of the lecture, he would close his notes and leave without even saying goodbye. I listened with profound sadness as this highly educated inspector volunteered his story.

There's teaching and there's teaching. If teaching was simply about imparting information then we'd only need the Internet… after all there's more information on the Net than we could digest in a 1,000 lifetimes. But most students and followers are not simply looking for information, they're looking for impartation of human touch, the stuff that's not just taught but caught. That sort of stuff comes from leaders and teachers who are both clever and connected!

People weren't just impressed by what Jesus taught, but by how He taught. He was a Rabbi like no other. He was brilliant and ordinary, holy but earthy, profound yet simple and most of all,

He did not only love the Torah, He loved the people to whom He taught the Torah!

When Jesus had finished saying these things, the crowds were amazed at His teaching, because He taught as one who had authority, and not as their teachers of the law.(18)

He understood people

I've had the privilege of visiting Israel on a number of occasions. On my last visit in February 2012, I went to Nazareth, the town Jesus grew up in. I say a town, for today Nazareth is a growing, busy place that bears no resemblance to the village Jesus grew up in 2,000 years ago. The Nazareth of Jesus' world had probably less than 300 residents and the synagogue where He gloriously declared, *"The Spirit of the Lord is upon Me..."*(19) is smaller than the foyer of our church, which meant that everyone would have not only been able to see and hear Jesus as He taught that day, but probably smelt His breath as well!

In such a place, living in tiny community, Jesus had the chance to study all of life with its challenges and joys as well as learn about different types of people. Though the metropolis of Jerusalem dwarfed Nazareth, and the Temple was bigger than the whole village itself, the people in both places were the same.

I confess to being a people watcher. Whether it's sitting in Starbucks or an airport lounge, I like to observe people (discreetly of course... lest they think me a stalker) and wonder what their story is, where they're coming from and where it is they're going. I remember arriving at the arrivals lounge to discover the young man due to pick me up had been delayed in traffic, so I decided to wait in the area of the lounge that gave me a great view of the meeting place, where passengers and family or friends reconnected. As I watched I observed a particularly beautiful young woman. She was clearly excited about meeting someone and by her dress code, I guessed it was a boyfriend or husband… Christmas was about to come early for him! After a few minutes the automatic doors swung open and out he came. I watched her reaction, one of joy, excitement and passion and then I saw his. He hardly cracked a smile. From his demeanour his bags looked really heavy and he made no attempt to get to her quickly. Undeterred she threw her arms around him, squeezing him tightly while he continued to hold onto the bags instead of grabbing the shapely woman. She persisted but the iceman refused to thaw. Suddenly she released him, he shrugged his shoulders pathetically, still holding the bags, and the two "lovers" headed for the exit. Christmas was cancelled!

Next time you read the gospels, check out the times Jesus notices people and details about them that others have missed. My granny used to say that "the devil is in the detail", but I think God's in the detail too, and Jesus was a detail person. He's great in front of a crowd, but He seems to reserve His best work for individuals and for people who felt that Jesus had truly noticed them. Where did He learn that skill? How easy it would have been for Jesus to want to escape to the city from the claustrophobia of the village, but not only did He stay, He learned, He engaged and in that tiny place of Nazareth in the region of Galilee, out of love for people, He learned about them, so He could understand them, so He could connect and communicate with them!

No one gets to be as good with people as Jesus was without giving time to love, live with and learn from those around them. Too many of us give in because we just don't get people, but Jesus refused to give up, persisting in His quest to know and be known. The thing you notice about the Jesus of the gospels is this: not only did Jesus like people, but they liked Him and even though

He wasn't understood by everyone, people somehow got Him, because He got them!

He invested in people

When Rabbi Jesus invited the crowd to take "His yoke", the culture in which He lived would have grasped immediately what He was saying.(20) Behind the image of the yoke lies two interrelated pictures. The first is an agricultural one – a sight common in Northern Israel. As farmers ploughed fields, they would do so, if wealthy enough, using oxen coupled together by a yoke; two working as one, moving in the same direction, sharing the same burden and connected for the same cause. The Rabbis picked this imagery up and would refer to their teaching or distinct philosophy as their "yoke". So to take the Rabbi's yoke was not simply to listen to his teaching, but to share his life. The yoked student wasn't just called to repeat the Rabbi's words, but reflect the Rabbi's life. At the heart of the Rabbi-student relationship is one of investment. The aim of the Rabbi was not simply to grow students, but develop leaders, people who could not only lead themselves, but bring leadership and guidance to others. The ambition of the Rabbi was to grow people big!

Jesus was a Rabbi. When He called His followers He promised, *"Come follow Me and I will MAKE YOU..."*(21) His agenda was not to take from them, but rather make them! His ambition was for Peter to emerge from Simon, the apostle of love to emerge from a young hot-headed bigot, a believer to emerge from a sceptic and a missionary to emerge from a zealot. Jesus the Rabbi sought to call greatness out of His young followers, so that they would go further than He ever managed.

As Jesus reclined in the home of a friend, a young woman sat at His feet to learn. We're not told what Jesus said or what questions she asked, but the image of Rabbi-student is unmistakable. Martha, the sister of Mary (the woman sitting at the feet of Jesus) was frantically trying to sort hospitality preparations. She was annoyed and expressed her disquiet at Mary. Jesus' reply is striking.

Martha, Martha, you are worried and upset about many things, but few things are needed – or indeed only one. Mary has chosen what is better, and it will not be taken away from her.(22)

Jesus was not saying Martha was wrong, but He was saying Mary was right... at that moment! Mary saw the Rabbi and wanted to get from Him all she could. The Rabbi recognised the heart of the student and refused to allow the opportunity to be lost. He saw the chance to invest in a woman hungry to learn and even at the risk of offending one of His dearest and most generous friends He continued to invest.

Jesus didn't attract people's favour because He glowed in the dark or floated around the streets or because He was Superman. I believe He attracted the favour of men because He did the human stuff really well. Long before He preached His first sermon or healed anyone, Jesus was doing the ordinary, human, people things. What we see in the three years of ministry is a fuller expression of the core values He learned in dead-end Nazareth. Jesus liked people, He learned about people and sought to genuinely understand them and He made it His goal to invest in them. Is it any wonder people liked Him?

It's too easy to conclude this genius is because Jesus was God, but Dr Luke points to an even more amazing truth: that even though He was God, He still learned, He deliberately grew and He invested Himself in knowing and loving those around Him.

If Jesus grew in favour with people... so can we!

Study & Reflection

"And Jesus grew in favour with man..."

Pick one of the four gospels and over the next week, read it the whole way through. While reading it, make a list of the following:

- Apart from the Jewish community, which was His main ministry focus, how many different racial groups does Jesus engage with and in what way does He do it?
- How many direct encounters are there with women and which one stands out to you... and why?
- Are there any specific examples of Jesus connecting with both wealthy people and the poor?
- How does Jesus engage with religious people?
- Find one example of Jesus connecting personally with someone on the margins (peasant, unclean and degraded, sick and expendables e.g. widows). How does He treat them and what is their response?

Read Luke 7:36-50
There are two main characters in the story apart from Jesus, Simon and the woman.

How does Jesus address and handle them both?

What do we learn about His awareness of people and His ability with people from this story?

From the gospel of Luke find two examples which demonstrate Jesus clearly liked people (or the people in question)?

If Jesus did give Himself to learn about people, what qualities does this suggest Jesus had?

Find and list three examples of Jesus directly investing into somebody.

Why not make reading through the gospels a regular part of your Bible reading program?

9. Leaving the Island

"And Jesus grew... in favour with man."
It was John Donne who penned the words:

> "No man is an island, entire of itself.
> Each is a piece of the continent, a part of the main."

However, leaving the island means learning to know and lead self, while also learning to know and engage with others. Goleman reminds us that we are often "...judged by how well we handle ourselves and each other,"(1) and if we are to follow Dr. Luke's trajectory, Jesus didn't just handle self and others well because He was God, but because He grew. Without the benefit of modern sociology, psychological or scientific expertise to inform Him, Jesus so grew in emotional intelligence that it became a powerful tool to enable Him to do what the Father wanted Him to do. In fact, as we look closer at the life of Jesus as represented in the Gospels, we see Jesus fulfilling three dynamic aspects of emotional intelligence as defined by modern research, standing as a model, instruction and inspiration to us, His followers.

Self-Awareness

Self-awareness has been defined as "...having a deep understanding of one's emotions, as well as one's strengths and limitations and one's values and motives."(2) Think of the moments when Jesus' behaviour was in deference to those around Him, when He was so aware of Himself that He was able to behave in a way that endeared Him to the people He was with, or allowed Him to engage more effectively in the context He was in. His self-awareness is seen in His ability to contend with so many different contexts, some of which would have been potentially uncomfortable for Him as a man, a Jew and a religious teacher.

Many years ago I came to a dramatic and transformational conclusion, that often I do not see the world around me as it is, rather I see it as I am! I realised that so much of what I saw was shaped not by external factors, but by my internal beliefs and mindscape. The journey to greater self-awareness, helped by family, friends and personality profiling tools, has enabled me to live healthier and, I hope, serve better. So often I blamed what was around me, when in truth it was due to paradigms within me, and sometimes I accused the devil of things that were really my fault.

I remember doing my first personality profiling exercise. I was a little nervous, not just because of the process but because the pentecostal world I was part of very much frowned on such things. I did the test and was going through the results with the expert when he said something that was a "eureka" moment for the rest of my life. Speaking of my personality type he said, "Remember, your personality profile is a preference not a prison." He further explained that my profile highlighted my personality *default*, my personality *home button* if you like, but even this could be trained, led and improved.

True self-awareness doesn't confine us to the prison house of "this is just the way I am". Rather, it empowers us to understand our natural and comfortable default. With the right support and skills, we can learn to manage those preferences to our personal advantage and the enhancement of the world around us.

Self-Management

Self-management has been defined as "…the component of EI (emotional intelligence) which frees us from being a prisoner to our feelings."(3) How often was Jesus the smartest person in the room and yet others were encouraged to learn? How often did He know what was in the hearts of those around Him, and yet He controlled His own responses? How often could Jesus have "cut loose" and yet He didn't snuff out the smouldering wick or break the bruised reed? Goleman concludes, "Out of control emotions can make smart people stupid,"(4) but when it comes to emotional intelligence Jesus was never that. He remained in control because He learned to manage His own feelings, thus He did not become a prisoner to them.

Self-management will allow us to acknowledge and even celebrate our feelings, but not be mastered by them to the extent that they set the tone of any context or derail an agenda. Self-management allows us to lead self well while protecting those we lead from being manipulated by our emotional incontinence. An awareness of how we are wired can empower us to manage that wiring better, without making it an excuse for inappropriate behaviour. As Goleman adds, "without knowing what we're feeling, we're at a loss to control those feelings. Instead our emotions control us."(5)

Jesus was emotional and it's okay for us to be too, but the challenge in growing in "favour with people", is to become aware of how we work, then bring that into submission to the Holy Spirit, as well as using it for the management of our own conduct.

Empathy

Empathy has been defined as "…understanding the issues or concerns that lie behind another's feelings."(6) As Goleman suggests, "others rarely tell us in words what they feel: instead they tell us in their tone of voice, facial expressions or other non-verbal ways."(7) Therefore, empathy at it best is "anticipating, recognising and meeting" the needs of those we serve or engage with.(8) How often do we see Jesus understand the feelings and concerns of those around Him and adjust His behaviour, tone and approach accordingly? He's firm and forthright but compassionate with Nicodemus, while in the very next chapter of John's Gospel, He makes Himself vulnerable to a Samaritan woman and perfectly times the moment He gives her a powerful word of knowledge, waiting until He has calmed her suspicion and fears. Though He's trying to win Nicodemus and the woman, in both cases, He adjusts His approach to help them because He understands them.

However, empathy does not come easily or quickly. It will only grow within us when we truly want to learn and know about the "concerns or feelings" of another. If we're not interested *in them*, we'll never empathise *with them*. This is why we must leave the island. Leaving the island where self is king and the world adapts to our desires is challenging, difficult and profoundly uncomfortable. But if like Jesus, we're prepared to grow in our understanding of others while learning to invest into them, then we will grow in empathy and our world will feel the difference.

If you've read my book *First Day*, then you'll be aware of my aversion to jigsaws. My wife Dawn loves them and I don't. She will take hours, even days, lovingly and painstakingly putting them together and I don't see the point of making something that's going to go back into the box! However, when it comes to getting a picture of the power of connectedness, the jigsaw has helped me no end. If you happen to have an old jigsaw in your home, why not dust it off and have it close to you while you read this chapter. As a visual aid it just might help connect the dots when it comes to being known and knowing!

Remember, we're thinking about the fact that Jesus grew in favour with people, in both His emotional wellbeing and

intelligence, and how He lived in such a way as to attract the favour
of those around Him. If we want to be followers and leaders who
authentically grow in our relationships and a greater awareness
of self and others, then we must leave the solitude and limitation
of the island and learn how to connect with those around us. As
we learn to know self, we grow in our knowing of others. Let's see
what the jigsaw teaches us about how to C.O.N.N.E.C.T.

Connectivity is essential

Take a look at any jigsaw, from 20 pieces (love them) to 1,000
pieces and you'll notice they have something in common. Every
piece of every jigsaw is designed to connect. Though there will be
a variety of styles, every piece will have been uniquely crafted to
fit with at least two other pieces. In fact it's impossible to be part
of the jigsaw and not connect!

When we look at God's engagement with humanity in the very
beginning, we're given an insight in the Creation story that can
fundamentally impact how we see our world and ourselves.

*"The Lord God said, 'It is not good for the man to be alone. I will
make a helper suitable for him.'"*(9)

Three things scream out here.

Firstly, the construction of the Hebrew emphasises the
negative phrase "not good" by placing it at the beginning of the
sentence, in contrast to the six "it was good" and one "it was very
good" contained in chapter one. God has just made creation and
declared it to be *good*, yet there is something within His perfect
creation that is declared to be *not good*. God is certainly not
saying the man is not good, rather it's the condition the man is in.
He is said to be "alone".

Secondly, the Hebrew word *băd*, translated "alone", points not
only to something or someone being alone, it implies the idea of

being apart. The context suggests an even stronger interpretation: that of being apart from something or someone that has the power to make the "alone" person complete, enabling them to fully function. So, God isn't saying the man is lonely, rather He's saying the man needs something or someone to make him whole!

Thirdly, the description of what we now know as the woman is striking. Note the language: "helper suitable for him". The word helper is *ēzer* and points to her indispensable role in achieving God's plan. The word does not imply someone who is lesser, either in this context or throughout the Old Testament, but rather a capable and competent helper or partner suitable for the task. (10) The woman was man's counterpart, corresponding to him. She would not only complete him emotionally and physically, but she would add to him all he needed to function effectively for God.

So what does all this mean? Just like the jigsaw piece, God designed us for connection. The Genesis account tells us plainly that it is impossible for any individual to do everything they were designed to do without connecting to helpers suitable for them. Too many in the pursuit of glory remain alone, using others instead of learning to partner with them. Like our first parents, we are called to leave the island of "aloneness" and learn to connect to others, because without such connection we cannot truly succeed. Connectivity is not an optional extra, it's absolutely essential to both our design and destiny!

One piece is not the whole picture

When buying a jigsaw, it normally comes in a box with the finished picture on the cover. Ah, how seductively alluring that is! As one glances at the picture, one forgets that 1,000 individual pieces have to be assembled to make it come alive. As the pieces are sorted (and my wife has a particular approach to sorting different pieces into different groups), one becomes aware of a simple but profound truth. No matter how beautiful, detailed or intricate any one piece may be, it is not and cannot be the whole picture. If that were the case, why would we need another 999 pieces?! It seems an attractive proposition that my picture is only ever about my piece, but just as the jigsaw designer has ensured no one piece gets all the glory, so has God.

God has designed us in such a way that when it comes to the particular pattern on our piece, it cannot be fully achieved just by concentrating on our one piece alone. His design ensures that no one piece can be complete alone, and that no one piece is the entire picture. Humanity wants to make it so, with the mantra of the *hyphenated self*, but God has always had another way. At times, the Bible is a glorious contradiction held in tension and this is seen so clearly when it comes to the individual. God celebrates the individual but never at the expense of community, and God champions community but never to the detriment of the individual. To get the best of both worlds, two worlds must become one! You're an important piece, but you're not the whole picture. Properly and soberly understand yourself while revaluing those around you, and I guarantee your picture will look better than it has ever done!

Nourish authentic friendships

On the rare occasions when I've ventured into the dark and murky world of the jigsaw, I have become frustrated at not being able to find the right piece. I remember trying to find one particular piece for over half an hour, by which time anything that resembled a Christian was leaking out of my body. In total desperation (and I'm really not making this up) I tried to make a piece fit by forcing it into the slot. The colours matched so I knew I was close. After my first attempt I knew it clearly didn't fit, but I was determined, "This sucker is going in!" A sharp rebuke from Dawn and I quickly volunteered to make some coffee!

The jigsaw taught me an important lesson that day: not any old fit will do... it has to be the right fit. This reminds us of the language of Genesis 2:18 which we've already considered. The woman wasn't any old fit, she was the right fit and that's why potentially both Adam and Eve, as they became known, could rule the earth, subdue the earth and fill the earth. Remember, the animal kingdom had been scoured for a potential partner for the man, but what was needed couldn't be found.

Most of us have many acquaintances, but that's not the same as friends. To nourish true friendships, and there won't be many that fall into this category, it will cost us in time. Without moving friendship to the top of the priority list and making sure it gets done, it will remain a great idea that could have been. We can't be friends with everyone, but we should be friends with someone, who like that jigsaw piece fits together well with us.

The price for friendship is high, but the cost of living life without authentic friendships is unthinkable. Friends cost T.I.M.E.

Trust – Without trust we know we have nothing because trust is at the heart of everything. In his book *The Speed of Trust*, Covey articulates a simple idea; that high trust leads to low cost which allows us to move fast. Think about the simplistic profundity of that for a moment. If in any relationship there is strong trust, then the cost between is low and we pay it willingly, which means we can move fast on any issue. But, of course, the opposite is true too! Low trust leads to high cost, which means we'll move slowly!(11)

Intimacy – David declared at the death of his dearest friend Jonathan, that Jonathan's love was more wonderful for him than that of a woman.(12) David found a level of emotional and relational intimacy with his friend that he hadn't found in any woman up to that time. This should not be understood in a sexual way, but rather in the purity of two hearts so connecting that, as men, they are open and safe with one another. What freedom such friendship brings, where we can be true, honest, authentic and vulnerable with another human being and know the details won't appear on Twitter or Facebook! Most crave this reality but few find it. In Swahili culture one can be greeted with the words, "I see you." Oh, to have friends who see us and love us just the same!

Movement – True friends will always provoke movement. As we engage with them "iron will sharpen iron" and we'll discover moments of conflict, friction and challenge taking place. I don't mean any of this in a negative or confrontational way, but in the route to true friendship, attitudes, actions, words and behaviour will come under scrutiny. One of the signs of authentic friendship is the moment of discomfort when a friend's example provokes our journey and when our attitude is comforted over lunch. True friends won't allow us to live in a never-land of unreality, they'll prod and provoke us to get into the real world and stay there!

Expense – All things of value cost and we are naïve to think that something of the value of true friendship can be acquired cheaply or in a "two for one" sale. We like the idea of a Rolex friendship at a knock-off price, but it never works. When it comes to friendship we are called to invest time, effort and even money to make sure we keep and grow what we have. People kill themselves for a car, a house or a holiday, and yet go cheap on friendship. Ultimately, our time card and our bank balance will reveal what we really believe in. Don't make friendship a budget item on your balance sheet because the returns on such an investment is usually huge.

Nurture productive partnerships

"Never omit any opportunity of getting acquainted with any good or useful man."(13)

I love this quote because of what we know about Wilberforce at the time. He was young, wealthy, powerful, influential and a rising star in the government, yet his attitude was one of enlargement, learning, growing and humility. His life, remembered largely for his heroic work on the abolition of slavery in Britain, was filled with variety, vibrancy and diversity. He pursued productive partnerships because he understood the power of the bigger picture.

A productive partnership is not necessarily a friendship as we've previously observed, but something which enables the completion of the picture. It's finding that piece which helps promote the greater cause so that more people get to see our colours on display. These partnerships could take a variety of forms.

Learning partnerships – something/someone that empowers you to grow and expand your learning and helps you to be better at what you do. Perhaps you want to learn about the New Testament more, then why not find a great teacher who'll give you an hour a week to learn? Maybe you want to improve your money skills, then seek out someone who can educate you on money. This partnership doesn't have to last forever, it may only be for a month or two, or even a year or two, but through it the big picture gets to the world.

Project partnerships – something/someone that enables a goal to be achieved that would have been impossible alone. I find churches and Christians can be much too proud in asking for help from those who have achieved a measure of success in a particular area. Why reinvent the wheel when it's already out there? Wouldn't it be better to work with those who have invented and found ways to use it? Today, I'm excited at the amount of genuine networking and partnership I see. Some of the old competitiveness has gone and today, certainly in the circles I move in, there is a desire to empower and enrich one another, using our resources and abilities in mutually beneficial ways.

Growing partnerships – something/someone that encourages you to grow into the God-given potential you already have. My dad is a keen gardener and over the years has won numerous trophies for his flowers. I've seen him tenderly nurture a flower to such beauty that when it's displayed, the stake which helped it to grow straight is long forgotten. We all need stakes planted beside us to help us grow; friends and partners that hold us to account and encourage us to grow straight.

Great partnerships don't just happen they have to be nurtured!

Every piece is elevated

The beauty of the jigsaw is that as it draws to completion something amazing happens: every piece gets a slice of the glory. Now it's true that some pieces will be celebrated more than others, and they'll draw the eye of the onlooker because they're central to the subject in the picture, but the reality is, even the "ordinary" pieces (the blue sky bits) are elevated because of their connectedness to the whole.

I have often said that the people around me make me look much better than I am. Through their contribution to my life, my gifts get to shine and the particular talents that God has given me get noticed. In serving me, I am elevated, and in that moment it is crucial that I do not forget how I got there and who made the vital contributions. If we are learning to truly connect to others every piece will experience uplift. Some pieces we're connected to get noticed more than us, because of their colours and talents in that particular context, but as they shine, so do we, and as they grow we also benefit.

Contributing not consuming

The subtle danger of being in a jigsaw is that we come to believe that the pieces we are connecting to are adding "to me". Although this is true, it is not the whole truth and there is a way of looking at it which allows the same action to take on a whole new dimension. What would happen if a jigsaw piece saw itself as "adding to others"? What if it had the courage to become a contributing jigsaw piece rather than a consumer piece? Someone might argue that it doesn't matter, because ultimately the connection occurs and the job is done, but in the world of the Kingdom, attitude is everything and has the power to transform every connection.

The reality for the jigsaw is that sometimes connecting to another piece adds more to the other than to you. For you, they might add another piece of that blue sky, but your contribution might add the one detail that makes their particular aspect of the picture complete. They've added to you, but you've enriched them!

So many live with a "what's in it for me" mindset, ensuring that every connection is poisoned by self-agenda and self-advancement. Their consumerism eclipses the shining light of contribution and an opportunity for growth and enlargement is lost. If, however, we can turn this mentality on its head, rather than diminishing we will increase. As Jesus said, "It's more blessed to give than to receive" because this is the way of the Kingdom and one which allows us to grow by giving not by grabbing. The world outside the Kingdom of God struggles to understand this philosophy. They have been schooled to grab, take, use and above all think of self above all others. In the Kingdom we're inspired to release, give, bless and think of others above self. It shouldn't work, but it does. When we live like this, we'll surely attract the favour of men!

Triumph flows from connection

What a wonderful moment when the jigsaw is complete. My wife has enjoyed this feeling many, many times, but outside of childrens' jigsaws (less than 50 pieces), this moment of euphoria has never been mine! Only then, do we see the power of connection. All the pieces have come together as one and in the beauty of the picture the joins fade into the background as everything mingles together in the big picture!

The Bible declares confidently,

"Two are better than one, because they have a good return for their labour: if either of them falls down, one can help him up. But pity anyone who falls and has no one to help them up. Also, if two lie down together, they will keep warm. But how can one keep warm alone. Though one may be overpowered, two can defend themselves. A cord of three strands is not quickly broken."(14)

Of course, two are only better than one if they work together as one. Two people working as two individuals will be better apart than together. Solomon shows us the power of connection in this lovely passage, so often read at weddings (and why not) but whose truths were also intended for life beyond matrimony. The passage shows us four aspects of the power of connection.

Synergy (v9) – when the energies of two synchronise as one, they will achieve more than the sum total of their parts. The biblical principle of synergy, found way back in Genesis 2:18 when the woman connected to the man's aloneness and two became one, teaches us that our productivity experiences multiplication not merely addition!

Do you have friends that multiply your energy?

Support (v10) – to fall in life in one form or another is inevitable, but what's not certain is what will happen when we do fall. Will we be left on the ground? Will we be kicked when we're down? Will we be judged for falling down? The tragedy of life is not that we fall, fail or slip, but that for so many, nobody cares to stop and help us to our feet.

Do you have friends who would pick you up if you fell?

Sustenance (v11) – Solomon uses the magnificent imagery of body warmth bringing sustenance on a cold night. Shivering alone in the cold soon saps our strength and destroys our resolve. To get any warmth at such a moment is good, but to get it from the heat of another person, so close to us that their heat becomes ours and our cold becomes theirs, is truly a glorious blessing. Such sustenance is personal, expensive and forever remembered!

Do you have friends who would sustain you in your need?

Strength (v12) – to recall a slogan I grew up with on the streets of Belfast, "united we stand, divided we fall". How true this is. No matter how strong we are, when we stand alone against an enemy the chances of our demise are high, but when we stand together it becomes much harder to overpower us. Why don't you experiment with the image of Solomon's words? Take a piece of thread and wrap it once around your fingers. Now open your fingers... I'm sure the thread will have snapped. Now use the same thread but wrap it around twice, three times and four times, until you can no longer open your fingers. What is surprising is how few times you have to wrap the thread. By itself it is vulnerable, but together, it's invincible.

Do you have friends who will stand and fight for you and with you?

Whatever you do, don't rush out and buy a jigsaw, but I urge you, don't ignore the lessons it screams at us. No one is an island, not even you. God not only wants you to leave the island but has given you the means to do so. With authentic self-awareness, greater self-management and genuine empathy, though the journey will feel a little scary, the rewards will be beyond our wildest dreams. We can learn to **C.O.N.N.E.C.T.** and grow in favour with people... if we want to.

As John Maxwell put it, "One is too small a number to achieve greatness."(15)

Study & Reflection

"And Jesus grew in favour with man..."

Before you start, get your hands on a jigsaw. You don't have to buy one, just borrow one if possible. Take out any piece and look at it carefully. Now write down everything you see and if you have them, let your study partner or group hear your findings. (If you're together in a group, everyone can do it).

Look at Genesis 2:18
Don't think about marriage or the relationship between a man and woman... just think community.

What does this verse say about our design?

What does it say about the type of relationships we should seek to have?

Why is it important to realise our piece is not the whole picture? How many authentic friends do you think you have and why do you consider them authentic? Do they line up with T.I.M.E.?

In what way does a partnership differ from a friendship? How can these be so powerful if nurtured properly?

In what areas or issues of your life would you like to develop an empowering partnership?

Read Ecclesiastes 4:9-12
Again, don't think marriage or man and woman, just think community.

What verse stands out to you or attracts you the most and why?

What are the biggest obstacles to finding this sort of friendship?

If you have great friends who fit into this chapter, why not take a moment to...

- Thank God for them.
- Thank them and be praise specific. Write them a card, send them an email or call them. Tell them how much they mean to you and how specifically they have enriched your life.

- Bless them. Why not treat them to something nice, something you know they'll like?

If you don't have great friends like this, then why not determine to leave the island.

- Ask God to give you great friends.
- Look around your church community and get connected to a small group, ministry or hobbies group.
- Don't get desperate, but do be diligent.

10. There Has to be a Reason

"And Jesus grew in wisdom and stature, and in favour with God and man."

As we come to the end of this book (but hopefully not the journey) let me remind you of its basic premise, captured in the profound simplicity of what I've called *the 2:52 principle*. As Jesus returns home with His earthly parents at the age of 12, He enters into 18 years of obscurity during which we know only a little about His life. However, Dr Luke gives us some insight when he tells us that Jesus grew (*prokóptō*) deliberately and intentionally. Jesus cut a path for growth towards a very definite destination. His growth was not merely natural or accidental, but rather pregnant with purpose. Jesus grew for a reason!

The four areas of His growth are striking in that together they represent a wholeness and completeness, which so prepares Jesus in the 91% that as a man, about to be empowered by the anointing of the Spirit, He is as ready as He could be.

Jesus grew in,

Wisdom – intellectually (IQ)
Stature – physically (PQ)
Favour with God – spiritually (SQ)
Favour with man – relationally (EQ)

Jesus grew in all these areas with intention and He grew in them for a reason. There was a reason behind and in everything that Jesus did. He wasn't just growing for the sake of growing; He grew for a reason, a purpose and towards a plan.

I love asking the "why" question, to myself and others. My mother said it was my most common question as a child (it must have been the teacher in me). When someone tells me they are going to do something I often ask why? Impressed as I might be by the particular endeavour, I'm always keen to know the motivation behind it, because I've come to understand that it's ultimately the motivation that keeps the idea moving.

I want to go to Bible School – why?

I want to get married – why?

I want to lose weight – why?

I want to leave this church – why?

I want you to mentor me – why?

I want to be rich – why?

We could go on and though it's an irritating question at times, it's one worth training yourself to ask of yourself and even of others. Why am I doing this? Why am I moving in this particular direction? Why do I have this job? The importance of this question is in forcing us to be clear, not so much on our ambition (the what), but our motivation (the why). I remember when I wanted to sign up for my Masters. Little did I know it would lead eventually to a PhD and seven years of continual postgraduate studies while leading a church and helping to raise a young family. I remember Dawn asking me why I wanted to do it. It forced me to clarify my reasons and move from the world of concept and dream to the world of reality. I had a reason and Dawn backed me 100% and now people call me Doctor! But there were moments during the long study hours, when everyone else was watching TV or chilling out and I was hammering away at the books or the keyboard of my computer, that I had to remind myself why I was doing it. When the second chapter of my PhD was returned and I was informed it needed a complete rewrite, having already written 6,000 words… I had to remind myself of why I was doing it. When Friday became known as PhD day in our home and I'd

disappear until I was finished, often working from 7am to 8pm…
I had to remind myself why I was doing it. The reason we do what
we do is important. We serve a Creator God who had the why
in place before He ever did anything and He has designed the
same code in each of us. Doing something is not enough… doing
something for a reason and for purpose is what each of us need!

In my book *First Day*, I talked about the fact that the Rabbis
used the term *melechet machshevet*: "work that involves the
realisation of thought, not mindless activity. It is labour guided
by a plan, directed towards a goal."(1) Jesus, the greatest Rabbi
who ever lived grew intentionally with a plan in mind, directing
His efforts towards a goal. If you and I are to learn to grow on
purpose, then we must find the purpose for which to grow. When
we find the purpose for growth, we will discover the motivation
to grow!

Growing on purpose

At the heart of Jesus' growth was an understanding of a greater
and bigger plan. As we observed in the opening chapter, even
at 12 He had an awareness and understanding of His destiny
referring to the Temple as His "Father's House". I suggest to you
that at the heart of His growth was an intimate relationship with
His Father and it's this which forms the engine room of why Jesus
does what He does.

When I met Dawn I was a 3rd year Bible student – and
I looked like one. My hair was probably a bit too long, I wore
jogging bottoms and an old baggy jumper a lot, and in truth,
apart from when on official duties, I wasn't overly concerned
about my appearance. After all I was there to "pursue my holy
calling" not have a relationship! However, Dawn changed all that.
As we grew closer I started to change, paying more attention to

my appearance and trying to look less like a student and possibly more like husband material. At the heart of the change was a person that I was coming to love and wanted to please. I had found a cause greater than the cost!

For a Jesus follower, the heart of learning to grow on purpose is a Person. I defy anyone who is truly getting close to the Presence of God not to feel the need to grow and develop in the things that God desires. The more we love Him the more we will want to please Him and out of that desire to please will be intentionality in growing in the ways that please and honour Him. Out of love for the Father there were no areas of Jesus' life out of bounds to growth and change – everything was about honouring Him and seeking to reflect Him in IQ, PQ, SQ and EQ. Jesus wasn't growing to position Himself in society, but rather to please the heart of God.

When we take growth seriously it's a sign we're taking God seriously!

Growing in purpose

As I write this chapter my three children are all at different and exciting stages of growth. My oldest daughter Elaina is about to move into her own place and take up a children's ministry post in her church. Simeon has just experienced the most incredible growth spurt over the last year and at 15 now stands six feet tall. Beth-Anne is about to leave the relative comfort of Junior school and go to High School where she'll have to make new friends and get used to lots of new things. All of them have grown enormously as people over the last few years, but this is just one snap-shot of their journey. If I write in another five years, I'll be describing another stage of their growth and hopefully they'll continue to grow until the day they die! As I've observed growing I've understood some powerful principles:

Growing produces change

Every time my kids grow, something has to change, whether it be clothes, the shape and style of their rooms or the way we live as a family. As much as we might want to, we can't stay the same and grow, it is simply impossible. Change in our lives is a sure sign we are growing.

Change provokes growth

Next week, I'll start the process of packing up the office I'm now writing in as we prepare as a family (without Elaina) to move to a new church. We've been at the Hub Christian Community fifteen years and have loved it here. But just over a year ago, God whispered a challenge that has produced total change in our family; new church, new house, new area, new schools, new accents, new title, new office, new challenges, new opportunities... means all change! However, all this change has provoked growth in us, from the emotional development of our children, to the wearing of a bigger ministry jacket and we've grown in prayer and seen again the miraculous provision and power of God. We're all bigger than we were six months ago and we haven't even moved yet!

Growing on purpose doesn't conclude at the end of a semester or with the award of a degree. Growing on purpose goes on and on and on and on! Those who seek to live in the dynamic of the 2:52 principle must recognise that growing is a Life-Long-Learning reality where we never really make it, we just progress to the next stage of development. Reading this book will not produce growth in you (although the fact you're reading it means you're serious about growing) but hopefully it will provoke growth in you.

Growing for purpose

Somebody once said that there are two great days in all our

lives, the day we were born and the day we discover why! None of us were born to merely exist and survive and yet that is the experience of billions of people. The Garden story of Genesis shows us that God made us out of love and for a purpose beyond ourselves. He wants us to know not only where we came from, but why we are here and where we are going. He longs for us to live in the power of purpose and all that brings to our lives.

Jesus lived for purpose.

I must proclaim the good news of the Kingdom of God to the other towns also, because that is why I was sent.(2)

My food is to do the will of Him who sent me and to finish His work.(3)

Jesus knew the purpose for which He had been sent and was able to tailor His life to fit that purpose. This morning before starting to write, I had to prepare our dining room for a decorator. It meant removing all the furniture, thus allowing him to get in easily and start the job. One of the jobs was taking the curtain poles down. They were held in place by star shaped screws which meant I had to go into the garage to my toolbox and find the screwdriver to fit the shape. I have about a dozen screwdrivers, but only one could do that particular job and fortunately I found it. All my screwdrivers look similar and roughly do the same job, but I needed a specific fit for that moment.

There is a fit for you. I know you look like a lot of other people and have similar skills to them, but God has a specific purpose for you to fulfil – one that will draw out the best of who you are and then highlight the unique contribution you can make to your world. Discovering this truly helps us to grow on purpose, just as knowing where we're going helps us to map out the journey. So many will struggle to grow on purpose because they're not sure of the purpose for which they were made. Hopefully this book will have further provoked that question and provided some guidance in finding the answers, if you haven't already done so.

When it comes to "learning to grow on purpose" it can all feel a little overwhelming. It's hard enough to grow in one area, but this book has outlined four areas in which Jesus grew and in which I've encouraged you to think about intentionally growing. So how can we do it… how can we grow in this way?

Make an elephant plan

"How does one eat an elephant? … One bite at a time!"

When it comes to growing on purpose we have to think one bite at a time, one step at a time and one day at a time. It's simple, but simple works, believe me. If we take enough bites the elephant will be eaten. If we walk enough steps the journey will be accomplished and if we live enough days, we'll end up enjoying an incredible life.

So what's the plan? I'm not going to give you a plan but some easy principles to help you make your own plan. I have mine, which works for my purpose and personality shape, and so to impose it on you would not be helpful, but I will give you the principles by which I build my plan.

- **Establish a purpose.** As Covey suggests, "begin with the end in mind." I know this is not easy, but think of where you'd like to be and what you think God wants it to look like and plan towards this. Design a vision statement and put it on your wall so that you can remind yourself why you are doing what you are doing. Remember, there has got to be a reason for everything.

- **Keep it practical.** Two keys words here:
  Attainable – whatever you design you have to be able to do! If you have three children under five, devotions around the

breakfast table might be an issue. If you've never exercised before, don't start with a ten-mile jog! Start with what you can do and build from there. If in all the areas you were able to do just one thing, that would be amazing... and a great place to start.

Sustainable – whatever you design you have to be able to keep doing it! I'd rather you read one chapter of the Bible every day for a year than aim to read ten and end up reading none. Better to have a "little and often" approach than "boom and bust". The issues of sustainability will be influenced by your world at any particular moment. Don't ignore the issues in your life, but build a plan that both works with them and starts to boss them.

- **Ensure it is profitable.** It is important that there is some level of profitability to everything we do. We may not notice the difference immediately, but we will eventually.

Two things can help here:

Aims – set yourself some targets on the different areas of IQ, PQ, SQ and EQ. These could be for three, six months or a year. You can go beyond a year, but these will tend to be for longer-term plans, such as finances and education. It's good to do this, but if you can hit the short-term goals, this will encourage you to set longer term targets.

Let me give you an example:

Three month plan:

IQ – I will read one book on the life of Jesus
PQ – I will go for a 20-minute power walk 3 times per week
SQ – I will read through the book of Proverbs, the gospel of

Luke and the book of Acts

EQ – I will have coffee (or dinner) with a friend(s) once per month

All of this is do-able, but the key is you've set yourself a definite goal for a specific period. You could have multiple targets within each section, as long as they are both attainable and sustainable!

Accountability – this is key to growth and there are two levels of accountability I want you to think about. Firstly, did I do what I set out to do? (e.g. the above plan) and secondly, what benefits am I experiencing as a result of this? Both of these you can do for yourself provided you can be both honest and objective, but it might be good to involve a friend at the beginning of the journey and then throughout the process, so they can ask you the important questions and give you a level of objectivity which might be helpful to you.

Whatever you do, start somewhere. If you're struggling to even put a plan together, that's where a good friend, leader or mentor might come in. They can help you cut the elephant up into bite-size lumps and help you to see that growing on purpose really is possible.

As we come to the end of this book it's important to remember we're not coming to the end of the journey. Thank you for reading it to the end and for having a desire to grow in the first place, undoubtedly the main reason you picked up this book. I pray that the 2:52 principle will become a friend to you, as it continues to be to me. I pray that you will know the joy of growing on purpose and see the joys and benefits of it. My heart's desire is that just like Jesus, you will learn to grow in wisdom, stature, and favour with God and people.

Study & Reflection

"And Jesus grew in wisdom and stature, and in favour with God and man."

Look at the four key areas, IQ, PQ, SQ & EQ. Would you say your growth in any or all of these has been intentional or accidental/random/haphazard?

The Rabbis talk of *melechet machshevet*: "work that involves the realisation of thought, not mindless activity. It is labour guided by a plan, directed towards a goal."

When it comes to the four areas in 2:52 how much of what you do is directed towards a goal, thus forming part of a bigger purpose?

Rate them on a scale of 1-10, 10 being excellent and 1 being poor.E.g. You might read a lot of books, but other than the love of reading there's no real purpose or plan to it, thus in this context that might score a 3 or 4.

IQ	1	2	3	4	5	6	7	8	9	10
PQ	1	2	3	4	5	6	7	8	9	10
SQ	1	2	3	4	5	6	7	8	9	10
EQ	1	2	3	4	5	6	7	8	9	10

(A score of 20 or over is moving in the right direction. Anything under 20 and you might need to be more intentional with what you do and why you do it.)

Do you have a plan?

Having read the book the main challenge now is to make an "elephant plan" if you haven't already done so.

The three keys to the plan:
- Establish a purpose
  Why am I doing what I'm doing?
- Keep it practical
  It needs to be attainable
  It needs to be sustainable
- Ensure it is profitable
  In this area it might be good to involve a friend who will help with the accountability in both incentive and objectivity.

Aims – 3 month, 6 month and 12 month goals. If you've never done it before, I'd encourage you to start with a 3 month goal, but try up to 3 possibilities in each area and see how you get on. For example, for three months:

PQ: – 20 minute power walk three times per week
         – No crisps and one bar of chocolate per week
         – Try to drink at least one bottle of water per day

Accountability – did you hit the targets and what benefit do you feel or see?

About the author

John has been in full-time Church leadership since 1987. Though called to the UK, John has ministered in over 40 nations of the world. As a leader, teacher and author John has a passion to equip and inspire leaders as well as empower followers of Jesus into effective lifestyle and service.

After leaving Bible School, he helped pioneer and repurpose a church in the village of Havercroft, West Yorkshire, serving there from 1987-1997. From Havercroft he moved to Rotherham New Life in South Yorkshire, where he helped repurpose that church into a vibrant missional community, serving from 1997-2012. In 2012 John joined the team of Renewal Christian Centre in Solihull, where he served as the Senior Associate Leader until the end of 2014. John also served as the Principal of the British Assemblies of God Bible College, leaving at the end of 2016. Based at New Life Scunthorpe (www.newlifechurch. uk), He also serves on the Apostolic Team of One Church where he supports their Network (www.weareone.church), whilst also travelling extensively engaging his passion to teach the Word of God, inspiring a generation of Jesus followers to love Him and serve their world.

A graduate of Mattersey Hall, he also holds a Masters degree in Pentecostal and Charismatic Studies from Sheffield University and a Doctorate from the University of Wales. He has authored thirteen books, Truthformation, Rest, Hope, Loved, Mission is Like a Box of Chocolates, Moving Beyond Mediocrity, Identity Theft, The real F word, First Day – Discovering the Freedom of Sabbathcentric Living, 2:52 – Learning to grow on Purpose, The Freedom of Limitation – Going beyond by Staying Within, Extravagant – When Worship becomes Lifestyle, Beyond Broken – finding power in the pain and his latest book Face to Face - from the tyranny of Pretence to the Freedom of Authenticity. (www.drjohnandrews.co.uk)

Born in Belfast, Northern Ireland, John is married Dawn and together they have three children, Elaina (married to Dan), Simeon and Beth-Anne, and a granddaughter, Abigail Willow, not forgetting Pepperoni and Salami (the sausage dogs). John's hobbies include supporting his beloved football team Liverpool, listening to music, reading and watching great movies. He loves to eat and among his favourite food groups are, Chinese, Thai and chocolate!

References

Chapter 1
Ready, Steady, Go!

1. Mark 6:3
2. Matthew 2:23
3. Luke 2:41-50
4. Luke 2:49
5. Galatians 4:4
6. Luke 1:20, Romans 5:6 & 9:9 respectively
7. R.T. France, *The Gospel of Mark : A commentary on the Greek text* (243). Grand Rapids, Mich.; Carlisle: W.B. Eerdmans; Paternoster Press 2002.
8. Andy Stanley, *Visioneering*, Multnomah Books, 1999, p.37.
9. *Mishnah* is a collection of the sayings and interpretations of Rabbis. Although it wasn't in written form until approximately 200 AD, it is accepted that the contents cover teaching over the previous 400 years thus covering the life of Jesus.
10. *Tanakh* is the name for the OT Scriptures and *Torah* covers the first five books of the OT, and means Instruction.
11. Ann Spangler & Lois Tverberg, *Sitting at the Feet of Rabbi Jesus*, Zondervan, 2009. Chapter 2, *Why a Jewish Rabbi*, gives excellent insights in the upbringing and learning of Jesus.
12. Stanley, Visioneering, p.8.

Chapter 2
How Did Jesus Get So Smart?

1. John 19:19-21
2. Malcolm Gladwell, *Outliers*, Penguin books, 2008, pp.35-68.
3. Kenneth E. Bailey, *Jesus through Middle Eastern Eyes*, SPCK, 2008, p.195.

Chapter 3
Life-long Learner

1. Matthew 4:19

2. Matthew 11:29-30

3. Mark Twain, *Taming the Bicycle*.

4. John Maxwell, *The 21 Irrefutable Laws of Leadership*, Maxwell Motivation Inc, 2006, p.24.

5. J. John & M. Stibbe, *A Barrel of Fun*, Monarch Books, 2003, p.62.

6. James 1:5-6 – He's the smartest Person to seek and smart people seek Him.

7. Bill Hybels, *Courageous Leadership*, Zondervan 2002, pp.181-183. Dee Hock's conclusions are from *The Art of Chaordic Leadership, Leader to Leader*, Winter 2000, p.22.

8. E.A. Nelson, *Spirituality and Leadership*, Navpress, 2002, p.84.

9. D.A. Garrett, *Vol. 14: Proverbs, Ecclesiastes, Song of songs* (electronic ed.). Logos Library System; The New American Commentary (87). Nashville: Broadman & Holman Publishers, 2001.

10. John 13:12-17

11. Luke 9:57-62

Chapter 4
Strong for the Journey

1. Robert J, Karris, *Eating your way through Luke's Gospel*, Liturgical Press, 2006, pp.4-5.

2. Luke 4:31

3. Luke 4:1-2, 14

4. Mark 1:13

5. Luke 22:44

6. John 19:30

7. John 19:30

8. Joshua 14:10-12

Chapter 5
The Spirituality of Physicality

1. 1 Timothy 4:8

2. 1Corinthians 3:16 (speaking of the corporate gathering) & 1 Corinthians 6:19 (the individual)

3. Nelson, Spirituality and Leadership, p.47.

4. Mark 6:31

5. For a detailed look at living in the power of rest, check out my book

First Day – discovering the freedom of sabbathcentric living, River Publishing, 2011. Also on Kindle.

6. Caroline Leaf, *Who Switched off My Brain*, Inprov, 2009, pp.125-130.

7. Wayne Cordeiro, *Leading on Empty*, Bethany House, 2009. His chapter entitled *Early Warning Signs* is excellent on spotting the signs and interpreting the warning lights.

Chapter 6
Learning to be Spiritual

1. N.T. Wright, *The New Testament for Everyone*, SPCK, 2011.
2. The New Testament Greek Commentary, The Gospel of Luke.
3. Luke 1:39-55
4. Psalms 23:6
5. Luke 3:22
6. Luke 3:23. My italics.
7. 1 John 3:1
8. Proverbs 30:23
9. Hebrews 5:8-9
10. Ecclesiastes 4:9
11. Genesis 11:6
12. Luke 7:1-10

Chapter 7
Inside Out

1. Proverbs 4:23 – my italics and emphasis
2. Romans 12:2 – my italics and emphasis
3. 3 John 3:2 – my italics and emphasis
4. John Maxwell, *The 21 Indispensable Qualities of a Leader*, Thomas Nelson Publishers, 1999, p.xi.
5. M.D. Miller, *The Kingdom Focused Leader*, Broadman and Holman Publishers, 2004, p.46.
6. Miller, *The Kingdom Focused Leader*, p.52.
7. Luke 6:48.
8. S.R. Covey, *The 7 Habits of Highly Effective People*, Simon & Schuster, 1989. Habit 1.
9. Covey, *The 7 Habits*, pp.18-32
10. Covey, *The 7 Habits*, p.15, quoting David Starr Jordan.

11. 1 Timothy 4:7

12. Maxwell, *The 21 Indispensable Qualities...* p.125.

13. Nelson, *Spirituality and Leadership*, p.171.

14. McNeal, op.cit., p.192.

15. Hybels, p.182.

16. Nelson, *Spirituality and Leadership*, p.84.

17. L.J. Michael, *Spurgeon on Leadership*, Kregel Publications, 2003, p.70.

18. Michael, *Spurgeon on Leadership*, p.99.

19. 1 Timothy 4:16

Chapter 8
A People Person

1. In my Bible the words of Jesus are in red.

2. Matthew 10:6

3. Matthew 8:5-13

4. John 4:1-42

5. John 12:20-22

6. Mark 7:24-30

7. Luke 8:1-3

8. Luke ch's 15, 18 & 21

9. Luke 10:38-42

10. Luke 13:16

11. Luke 24:5-10 (they were called to remember His words)

12. Karris, *Eating*, p.97.

13. Luke 5:29-32; 7:34; 15:1-2 & 19:1-10

14. Luke 7:36; 11:37 & 14:1

15. J.M. Arlandson, *Women, Class, and Society in Early Christianity*, (USA: Hendrickson, 1997), pp.120-126.

16. Karris, *Eating*, p.27.

17. John 3:16

18. Matthew 7:28-29

19. Luke 4:18

20. Matthew 10:28-30

21. Matthew 4:19, my capitals

22. Luke 10:38-42, my italics

Chapter 9
Leaving the Island

1. Daniel Goleman, Working with Emotional Intelligence, , Penguin Random House, USA, 1999, p.1
2. Daniel Goleman, The New Leaders: Transforming the Art of Leadership, Time Warner, USA, 2003, p.106
3. Goleman, The New Leaders, p.57 - My brackets
4. Goleman, Working with... p.22
5. Goleman, The New Leaders, p.56
6. Goleman, Working with... p.135
7. Goleman, Working with... p.135
8. Goleman, The New Leaders, p.151
9. Genesis 2:18
10. God is seen as ʿēzer for example in Exodus 18:4 and Ps.121:1-2
11. Stephen M.R. Covey, *The Speed of Trust, the one thing that changes everything*, Simon & Schuster UK Ltd, 2006.
12. 2 Samuel 1:26
13. William Hague, *William Wilberforce, the life of the great anti-slave trade campaigner*, Harper Collins, 2007, p.201. A word of advice to his son Samuel.
14. Ecclesiastes 4:9-12
15. John C. Maxwell, *The 17 Indisputable Laws of Teamwork*, 2001, p.1.

Chapter 10
There Has to be a Reason

1. *First Day – discovering the freedom of sabbathcentric living*, River Publishing, 2011, p. 27.
2. Luke 4:43
3. John 4:34

Made in the USA
Las Vegas, NV
25 October 2021